SECOND EDITION

2

INSIDE READING

The Academic Word List in Context

Lawrence J. Zwier

SERIES DIRECTOR:

Cheryl Boyd Zimmerman

OXFORD
UNIVERSITY PRESS

OXFORD
UNIVERSITY PRESS

198 Madison Avenue
New York, NY 10016 USA

Great Clarendon Street, Oxford, OX2 6DP, United Kingdom

Oxford University Press is a department of the University of Oxford.
It furthers the University's objective of excellence in research, scholarship,
and education by publishing worldwide. Oxford is a registered trade
mark of Oxford University Press in the UK and in certain other countries

General Manager, American ELT: Laura Pearson
Publisher: Stephanie Karras
Associate Publishing Manager: Sharon Sargent
Development Editor: Keyana Shaw
Director, ADP: Susan Sanguily
Executive Design Manager: Maj-Britt Hagsted
Electronic Production Manager: Julie Armstrong
Senior Designer: Yin Ling Wong
Designer: Jessica Balaschak
Image Manager: Trisha Masterson
Production Coordinator: Brad Tucker

ISBN: 978 0 19441628 3 STUDENT BOOK

Printed in China

This book is printed on paper from certified and well-managed sources

ACKNOWLEDGEMENTS

*The authors and publisher are grateful to those who have given permission to reproduce
the following extracts and adaptations of copyright material*:

Illustrations by: p. 3 Infomen; p. 9 Infomen; p. 42 Barb Bastian; p. 73 Infomen; p.
74 John Kaufman; p. 106 Infomen; p. 147 Infomen..

*We would also like to thank the following for permission to reproduce the following
photographs*: Cover: Mary Evans Picture Library/Alamy (portrait); Stockbyte/
Getty Images (weathervane); Janis Christie/Getty Images (Barometer);
Chris Rady/Getty Images (avocado); Creative Crop/Getty Images (handbag);
James Lauritz/Getty Images (bulldozer); Carlina Teteris/Getty Images (bee);
Marilyn Volan/Shutterstock (diamonds); Suto Norbert Zsolt/Shutterstock
(wallnuts); TSI Graphics (map); Rstem Grler/iStockphoto (iMac); Stephen
Krow/iStockphoto (iPhone); pg. xii, Marcin Krygier / iStockphoto (laptop); p.
1 3d brained/Shutterstock; p. 3 Don Donovan Photography; p4 David Wall/
Alamy; p. 9 Logan Mock-Bunting/Getty Images; p. 10 Hemera/Thinkstock;
p. 17 Motoring Picture Library/Alamy; p. 19 Robert Patterson/Getty Images
(motorbike); p. 19 Motoring Picture Library/Alamy (car); p. 26 Ronald Grant
Archive; p. 33 gualtiero boffi/Shutterstock; p. 34 Ocean/Corbis UK Ltd.; p.
35 imagebroker/Alamy; p. 41 RichardBakerBA/Alamy; p. 49 iStockphoto/
Thinkstock; p. 50 GL Archive/Alamy; p. 51 Mary Evans Picture Library/Alamy
(de Vere); p. 51 c.Col Pics/Everett/Rex Features (queen); p. 57 Pictorial Press Ltd/
Alamy; p. 58 Hulton Archive/Getty Images; p. 65 iStockphoto/Thinkstock; p.
66 NASA - Goddard Space Flight Center (GSFC); p. 67 INSADCO Photography/
Alamy; p. 81 Alex Staroseltsev/Shutterstock; p. 82 Prisma Bildagentur AG/
Alamy (saturated fats); p. 82 Koeb, Ulrike/the food passionates/Corbis UK Ltd.
(unsaturated fats); p. 83 DR MARK J. WINTER/Science Photo Library; p. 90
US Civilian Public Service; p. 91 Wallace Kirkland/Time Life Pictures/Getty
Images; p. 97 Science Photo Library; p. 98 Map Resources/Shutterstock; p.
105 Titti Soldati/Alamy; p. 113 urfin/Shutterstock; p. 114 Dew/Somos Images/
Corbis UK Ltd.; p. 115 PhotoSpin, Inc/Alamy; p. 122 Image Source/Getty
Images; p. 123 AbleStock.com/Thinkstock; p. 129 majeczka/Shutterstock (blue
sky); p. 129 WDG Photo/Shutterstock (sunset); p. 130 DreamPictures/Getty
Images; p. 131 Image Source/Corbis UK Ltd.; p. 137 Gtranquillity/Shutterstock
(original); p. 137 Gtranquillity/Shutterstock; p. 138 Oxford University Press; p.
145 Antagain/iStockphoto; p. 146 NHPA/Photoshot; p. 153 Alex Wild/Visuals
Unlimited/Corbis UK Ltd.; p. 154 Phil Degginger/Alamy.

*The publisher would like to thank the following for their permission to reproduce the
following extracts and adaptations of material. Every effort was made to contact the
rights holders of extracted and adapted material. Please contact the publisher regarding
any rights ownership queries*: p. 3 Adapted from "Opal Fever: Adventures in the
Outback" by Kathy Marks, March 10, 2002, Travel section, The Independent.
Reprinted by permission of The Independent; p. 8 Adaptation of "The Ugly
Underneath" by Amanda Gefter, Philadelphia City Paper, Sept. 7-13, 2006.
Reprinted by permission of City Paper; p. 19 Excerpt from "Maintaining
Harley Davidson's Allure," interview by Kai Ryssdal with Jim Ziemer,
Marketplace PM, NPR, August 7, 2006. Reprinted by permission of Minnesota
Public Radio; p. 69 Average temperature and precipitation chart for Moscow,
climatetemp.info/russia/moscow.html; p. 76 Adapted from earthobservatory.
nasa.gov; p. 84 From Kannas et al. (2009), "Maternal Levels and Toddler Free-
Play Attention." Developmental Neuropsychology, 34:159-174. Department
of Psychology, Loyola University, Chicago; p. 90 "They Starved So that Others
Be Better Fed: Remembering Ancel Keys and the Minnesota Experiment," by
Leah M. Kalm and Richard D. Sembal. J Nutr (2005; 135:6), American Society
for Nutrition. Reprinted by permission; p. 99 Adapted from U.S. Geologic
Survey, "Plate Tectonics" at http://pubs.usgs.gov; p. 105 Adapted from Xan
Rice, "In the land of death, scientists witness the birth of a new ocean" The
Guardian, November 2, 2006. Reprinted by permission of The Guardian; p.
105 From "The Latest Leakey Searches for Our Earliest Ancestors," interview
with Maeve Leakey, California Wild magazine, Summer 1999. Vol 52:3; p. 114
Adapted from "Judging Roommates by their Facebook Cover," Elizabeth F.
Farrell, The Chronicle of Higher Education, Sept. 1, 2006. Copyright 2006, The
Chronicle of Higher Education. Reprinted with permission; p. 122 "Terror in
Littleton: The Teenage Culture; Arizona High School Provides Glimpse Inside
Cliques' Divisive Webs," by Tamar Lewin. From The New York Times, 5/2/1999
© 1999 The New York Times. All rights reserved. Used by permission and
protected by the Copyright Laws of the United States. The printing, copying,
redistribution, or retransmission of this Content without express written
permission is prohibited; p. 137 Adapted from Jim Lewis, "Don't Believe What
You See in the Papers: The Untrustworthiness of News Photography." Accessed
November 2006 at http://slate.com/id/2147502. Reprinted by permission of Jim
Lewis; p. 153 From Bitten: True Medical Stories of Bites and Stings by Pamela
Nagani, MD, copyright © 2004 by the author and reprinted by permission of
St. Martin's Press, LLC.

Acknowledgements

We would like to acknowledge the following individuals for their input during the development of the series:

Amina Saif Mohammed Al Hashamia
College of Applied Sciences – Nizwa, Oman

Amal Al Muqarshi
College of Applied Sciences – Ibri, Oman

Dr. Gail Al-Hafidh
Sharjah Women's College –
Higher Colleges of Technology, U.A.E.

Saleh Khalfan Issa Al-Rahbi
College of Applied Sciences – Nizwa, Oman

Chris Alexis
College of Applied Sciences – Sur, Oman

Bernadette Anayah
Folsom Lake College, CA, U.S.A.

Paul Blomeyer
King Fahd Naval Academy, Jubail,
Kingdom of Saudi Arabia

Judith Buckman
College of Applied Sciences – Salalah, Oman

Peter Bull
Abu Dhabi Men's College –
Higher Colleges of Technology, U.A.E.

Bjorn Candel
Fujairah Men's College –
Higher Colleges of Technology, U.A.E

Geraldine Chell
Sharjah Women's College –
Higher Colleges of Technology, U.A.E

Hui-chen Chen
Shi-lin High School of Commerce, Taipei

Kim Dammers
Golden Bridge Educational Centre, Mongolia

Steven John Donald
Waikato Institute of Education, New Zealand

Patricia Gairaud
San Jose City College, CA, U.S.A.

Joyce Gatto
College of Lake County, IL, U.S.A.

Sally Gearhart
Santa Rosa Junior College, CA, U.S.A.

Dr. Simon Green
Colleges of Applied Sciences, Oman

Andrew Hirst
Sharjah Women's College –
Higher Colleges of Technology, U.A.E

Elena Hopkins
Delaware County Community College, DE, U.S.A.

William Hussain
College of Applied Sciences – Sur, Oman

Tom Johnson
Abu Dhabi Men's College –
Higher Colleges of Technology, U.A.E.

Sei-Hwa Jung
Catholic University of Korea, South Korea

Graham Martindale
SHCT Sharjah Higher –
Colleges of Technology, U.A.E.

Mary McKee
Abu Dhabi Men's College –
Higher Colleges of Technology, U.A.E.

Lisa McMurray
Abu Dhabi Men's College –
Higher Colleges of Technology, U.A.E.

Sally McQuinn
Fujairah Women's College –
Higher Colleges of Technology, U.A.E.

Hsieh Meng-Tsung
National Cheng Kung University, Tainan

Marta Mueller
Folsom Lake College, RCC, CA, U.S.A.

Zekariya Özşevik
Middle East Technical University, Turkey

Margaret Plenert
California State University, Fullerton UEE,
American Language Program, CA, U.S.A.

Dorothy Ramsay
College of Applied Sciences –
Sohar, Oman

Cindy Roiland
College of Lake County, IL, U.S.A.

Elia Sarah
State University of New York
at New Paltz, NY, U.S.A.

Rachel Scott
Sharjah Women's College –
Higher Colleges of Technology, U.A.E.

Tony Sexton
Abu Dhabi Men's College –
Higher Colleges of Technology, U.A.E.

Siân Walters
Sharjah Men's College –
Higher Colleges of Technology, U.A.E.

Martin Weatherby
St. Thomas University, Japan

Contents

An Insider's Guide to Academic Reading

Develop reading skills and aquire the Academic Word List with
Inside Reading Second Edition.

Student Books

iTools for all levels

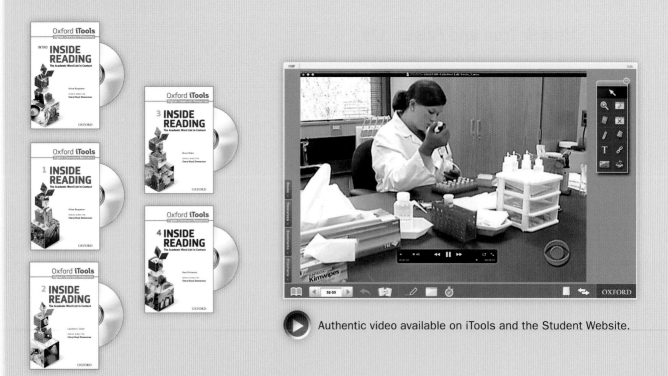

Authentic video available on iTools and the Student Website.

Getting Started

Each unit in *Inside Reading* features

> **Two high-interest reading texts** from an academic content area

> **Reading skills** relevant to the academic classroom

> Targeted words from the **Academic Word List**

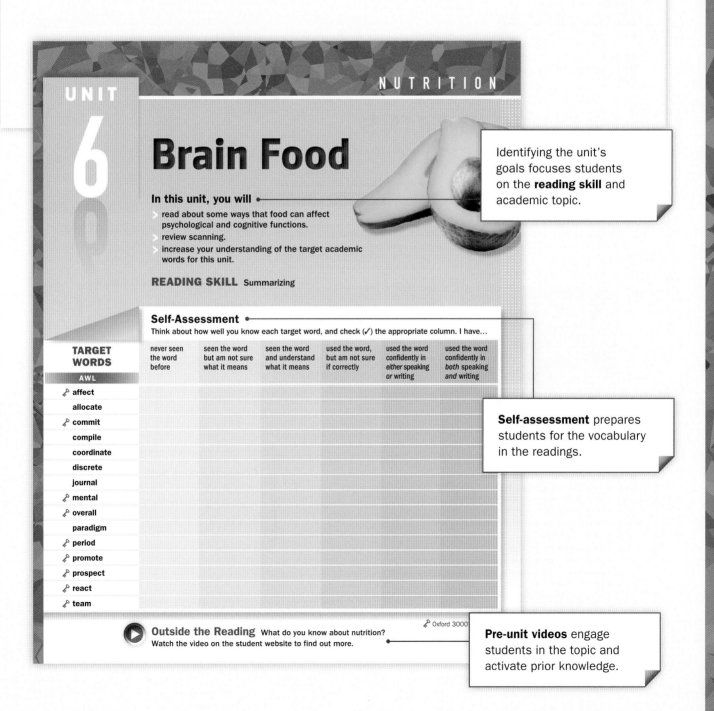

UNIT

6

NUTRITION

Brain Food

In this unit, you will

> read about some ways that food can affect psychological and cognitive functions.

> review scanning.

> increase your understanding of the target academic words for this unit.

READING SKILL Summarizing

Identifying the unit's goals focuses students on the **reading skill** and academic topic.

Self-Assessment

Think about how well you know each target word, and check (✓) the appropriate column. I have...

TARGET WORDS	never seen the word before	seen the word but am not sure what it means	seen the word and understand what it means	used the word, but am not sure if correctly	used the word confidently in *either* speaking *or* writing	used the word confidently in *both* speaking *and* writing
AWL						
🔑 affect						
allocate						
🔑 commit						
compile						
coordinate						
discrete						
journal						
🔑 mental						
🔑 overall						
paradigm						
🔑 period						
🔑 promote						
🔑 prospect						
🔑 react						
🔑 team						

Self-assessment prepares students for the vocabulary in the readings.

▶ **Outside the Reading** What do you know about nutrition? Watch the video on the student website to find out more.

🔑 Oxford 3000™

Pre-unit videos engage students in the topic and activate prior knowledge.

High-interest Texts

Before You Read •————

Read these questions. Discuss your answers in a small group.

1. Name three or four foods you often eat even though you know they're not good for you. Why are they unhealthful? Why do you eat them anyway?

2. Name three or four foods you eat that are healthful. Why are they healthful? Do you like the way they taste?

3. Have you ever felt a significant improvement in your mood or in your concentration after a meal or snack? What do you think caused this effect?

MORE WORDS YOU'LL NEED
cognitive: related to thought and learning
diet: the set of foods a person usually eats
intolerant: unwilling or unable to accept certain behavior or circumstances

🔊 **Read** •————

This excerpt from a nutrition manual explains the psychological benefits of eating certain fats.

> Discussion questions activate students' **knowledge** and prepare them to read.

> High-interest readings motivate students.

FAT FOR BRAINS

As the old saying goes, you are what you eat. The foods you eat obviously **affect** your body's performance. They may also influence how your brain handles its
5 tasks. If it handles them well, you think more clearly, and you are more emotionally stable. The right foods can help you concentrate, keep you motivated, sharpen your memory, speed your **reaction** time, reduce stress, and perhaps
10 even prevent brain aging.

GOOD AND BAD FAT
Most people associate the term *fat* with poor

health. We are encouraged to eat fat-free foods and to drain fat away from fried foods. To understand its nutritional benefits, however, we
15 have to change the **paradigm** for how we think about fat.

The first step is gaining a better understanding of fat. Instead of conceiving of it as a single thing, we have to recognize it as several
20 **discrete** types of a similar compound. Not every fat is your enemy. Fats—the right kinds and in the right amounts—are among your best friends. It is smart to **commit** to a balanced-fat diet, not to a no-fat diet.

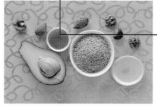

Foods high in saturated fats   Foods high in unsaturated fats

> Academic Word List vocabulary is presented in context.

82 UNIT 6

Reading Comprehension •————

Mark each sentence as *T* (true) or *F* (false) according to the information in Reading 1. Use the dictionary to help you understand new words.

___ 1. Foods affect a person's moods and motivation.

___ 2. Ideally, more people should commit to no-fat diets.

___ 3. At room temperature, you could pour unsaturated fat out of a bottle.

___ 4. It is not healthful to eat a very large amount of unsaturated fat.

___ 5. Omega-3 fatty acids promote intellectual development.

___ 6. A study showed that children born from high-DHA mothers are better able to pay attention.

___ 7. Research journals reported that people with a lot of omega-3 fats in their systems were very depressed.

___ 8. Patients with psychological problems should coordinate their therapy so that it includes dietary as well as psychological treatment.

> Comprehension activities help students understand the text and apply the targeted academic vocabulary.

Explicit Reading Skill Instruction

READING SKILL — Highlighting and Annotating

LEARN

After you read an article or chapter in a book, you may need to refer to the information again; for example, when you're studying for a test or writing an essay. Instead of copying the information you might need into a notebook, it is more efficient to *highlight* and *annotate* the reading.

Highlighting   Use a bright marker to make important passages easy to see. You might also want to underline or circle parts of the reading.

Annotating   Write little notes to yourself in the margins of the reading.

Highlight and annotate only the materials that you own! If you are borrowing a book, do not write in it.

APPLY

Follow the directions to highlight and annotate Reading 1. You will need a colored marker and a pen or pencil. Then, with a partner, use your annotations to answer the questions that follow as quickly as you can.

- First, highlight all the names of individual people.
- Second, circle each name of a college or university. In the margin next to each, write its location.
- Third, highlight or underline any statistics or important data in the article (look for numbers and source citations).
- Fourth, as you read, highlight any unfamiliar words you encounter. In the margin next to each, write a short definition using your dictionary.

> **Explicit reading skills** provide the foundation for effective, critical reading.

> **Practice exercises** enable students to implement new reading skills successfully.

APPLY

Follow the directions to highlight and annotate Reading 1. You will need a colored marker and a pen or pencil. Then, with a partner, use your annotations to answer the questions that follow as quickly as you can.

- First, highlight all the names of individual people.
- Second, circle each name of a college or university. In the margin next to each, write its location.
- Third, highlight or underline any statistics or important data in the article (look for numbers and source citations).
- Fourth, as you read, highlight any unfamiliar words you encounter. In the margin next to each, write a short definition using your dictionary.

1. What school is Brandi going to attend? _____
2. Where is Denison University? _____
3. How many registered users does Facebook have? _____
4. Where do most of Orkut's users live? _____
5. What other networking site is mentioned in the article? _____
6. What does *posturing* mean in this context? _____
7. Which musicians do Brandi and Sarah both like? _____
8. Who is the dean of students at Denison University? _____

REVIEW A SKILL   Finding the Main Idea (See p. 20)

Look again at Reading 1. Find the main idea of each section of the reading. In sections 2, 3, and 4, the main idea is not the same as the heading.

1) Paragraph 2
2) "Roomate Research"
3) "Prevention Beats Intervention"
4) "Brandi and Sarah"

> **Recycling of reading skills** allows students to apply knowledge in new contexts.

The Academic Word List in Context

Based on a corpus of 3.4 million words, the **Academic Word List (AWL)** is the most principled and widely accepted list of academic words. Compiled by Averil Coxhead in 2000, it was informed by academic materials across the academic disciplines.

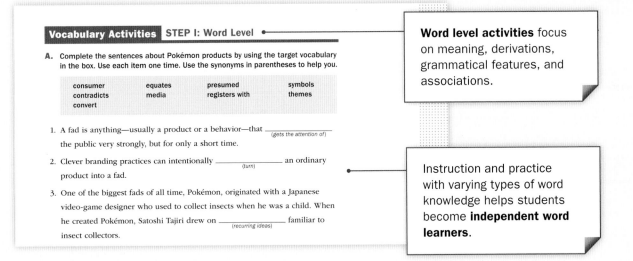

Vocabulary Activities STEP I: Word Level

A. Complete the sentences about Pokémon products by using the target vocabulary in the box. Use each item one time. Use the synonyms in parentheses to help you.

consumer	equates	presumed	symbols
contradicts	media	registers with	themes
convert			

1. A fad is anything—usually a product or a behavior—that _____ *(gets the attention of)* the public very strongly, but for only a short time.

2. Clever branding practices can intentionally _____ *(turn)* an ordinary product into a fad.

3. One of the biggest fads of all time, Pokémon, originated with a Japanese video-game designer who used to collect insects when he was a child. When he created Pokémon, Satoshi Tajiri drew on _____ *(recurring ideas)* familiar to insect collectors.

> **Word level activities** focus on meaning, derivations, grammatical features, and associations.

> Instruction and practice with varying types of word knowledge helps students become **independent word learners**.

Vocabulary Activities STEP II: Sentence Level

Word Form Chart			
Noun	**Verb**	**Adjective**	**Adverb**
accumulation	accumulate	accumulated	_____
author	author	authorial	authorially
debate	debate	debatable	debatably
sustenance sustainability	sustain	sustainable sustained	sustainably
volume	_____	voluminous	voluminously

D. Read another article about Shakespeare's works. Then restate the sentences in your notebook, using the words in parentheses. Be prepared to read aloud or discuss your sentences in class.

1. After Shakespeare's death, actors John Heminge and Henry Condell collected copies of his plays. (*author*)

   *After Shakespeare's death, Heminge and Condell collected copies of the **author**'s plays.*

2. Within seven years of Shakespeare's death in 1616, they had put together one of the landmark publications in English literature, the *First Folio*. It contained 36 of his plays. (*voluminous*)

> **Vocabulary work progresses** to sentence level and focuses on collocations, register, specific word usage, and learner dictionaries.

From Research to Practice

The Oxford English Corpus provides **the most relevant and accurate picture of the English language**. It is based on a collection of over two billion carefully-selected and inclusive 21st century English texts.

As an adjective, the word *medium* refers to anything that is not large and not small, but somewhere between, as in "a person of medium height."

As a noun, however, *medium* has a completely different meaning. It refers to a way to convey or send something. The plural form is *media*.

*Some chemical reactions require a **medium** to help them take place.*

*Television and radio are popular **media** for getting the news.*

CORPUS

B. What is each of these things a medium for? List as many things as you can. Discuss your ideas with a partner.

1. a newspaper: _____

2. the telephone system: _____

3. a letter: _____

4. the postal service: _____

5. the Internet: _____

6. gossip: _____

The verb *subsidize* means "to give money to someone or an organization to help pay for something." The noun is *subsidy*.

*The city **subsidizes** ambulance companies in order to keep the price of their services low.*

*These companies could not continue to operate without **subsidies** from the city.*

CORPUS

C. Read these pairs of items. With a partner, write down some ways that the first item might subsidize the second. Then, in a small group, discuss whether you think the subsidies should exist or should continue. Give reasons for your opinions.

1. parent / child's education: _____

2. government / students: _____

3. government / small businesses: _____

4. employer / employee's healthcare: _____

5. employer / employee's education: _____

6. local government / rent: _____

Corpus-based examples from the **Oxford English Corpus** of American English. Real-life examples help students learn authentic English.

Resources

STUDENT SUPPORT

For additional resources visit:
www.oup.com/elt/student/insidereading

> **Reading worksheets** provide additional skill practice
> **Videos** set the stage for specific units
> **Audio recordings** of every reading text

TEACHER SUPPORT

The *Inside Reading* **iTools is for use with an LCD projector or interactive whiteboard.**

Resources for whole-class presentation

> Audio **recordings** of all **reading texts with "click and listen"** interactive scripts
> **Animated presentations** of reading skills for whole class presentations
> **Videos** for specific units introduce students to the reading text topic and activate prior knowledge.
> **Fun vocabulary activities** for whole-class participation

Resources for assessment and preparation

> Printable worksheets for **extra reading skill practice**
> Printable and customizable **unit, mid-term, and final tests**
> Answer Keys
> Teaching Notes
> Video transcripts

Additional resources at:
www.oup.com/elt/teacher/insidereading

UNIT 1

Going Underground

In this unit, you will

> read about the benefits of living and working underground.
> learn how one metropolitan city uses technology to determine what exists underneath it.
> increase your understanding of the target academic words for this unit.

READING SKILL Previewing and Predicting

Self-Assessment

Think about how well you know each target word, and check (✓) the appropriate column. I have...

TARGET WORDS	never seen the word before	seen the word but am not sure what it means	seen the word and understand what it means	used the word, but am not sure if correctly	used the word confidently in *either* speaking *or* writing	used the word confidently in *both* speaking *and* writing
AWL						
🔑 assume						
🔑 create						
🔑 emerge						
🔑 environment						
🔑 ethnic						
immigrate						
🔑 liberal						
🔑 locate						
notwithstanding						
🔑 predict						
🔑 similar						
🔑 structure						
🔑 technique						
🔑 unique						

🔑 Oxford 3000™ keywords

Outside the Reading What do you know about engineering?
Watch the video on the student website to find out more.

Before You Read

Read these questions. Discuss your answers in a small group.

1. Where is Australia? What do you know about its weather and its landscape?

2. Have you ever seen a movie or a photograph showing a mine? If so, describe what you saw. If not, what do you think conditions in a mine are like?

3. Would you like to live in an underground house? Why or why not?

READING SKILL | Previewing and Predicting

LEARN

Previewing and *predicting* are strategies you can use before you read a text. A quick preview of the key elements of a text can help you predict what it might be about. This will help prepare you to take in the information as you read.

To preview a text:

- Read the title and any headings.
- Look at any photographs, illustrations, or graphics.

Then, based on your preview, predict some ideas and information you expect to find in the text.

APPLY

Take one minute to preview Reading 1. In the first column of the chart, write five words or phrases that caught your attention during your preview. In the middle column, use each word or phrase to create a prediction about the reading.

Word or phrase	Prediction	Accurate?
1. Down under	The reading will be about Australia.	

After you read, write *Y* (yes) next to each accurate prediction and *N* (no) next to each inaccurate prediction in the last column of the chart. Write a question mark (?) if you are not sure. Discuss your results with the class.

🔊 Read

This online travel magazine article is about a town in Australia's outback, or isolated rural areas, where underground homes are common.

○ ○ ○

Coober Pedy: Really Down Under

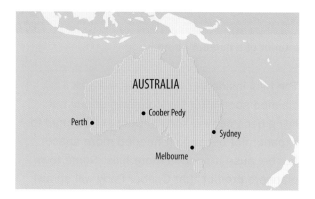

Coober Pedy, a dusty town in South Australia, sits atop the world's greatest known deposits of opal—a milky white gem with stripes and flecks of color. In hopes of getting rich, gemstone
5 miners endure the harsh outback **environment**. They suffer through dust storms, flies, and midsummer temperatures higher than 120° Fahrenheit (about 50° Celsius). To escape the heat and the flies, the people of Coober Pedy go
10 underground. They carve homes—called "dug-outs"—into the hills overlooking the town. Subterranean[1] living has become normal in Coober Pedy. There are shops, hotels, meeting halls, and restaurants underground.

THE MINERS ARRIVE

15 The first opals in Coober Pedy were discovered by a 14-year-old boy, Willie Hutchinson, who was looking for gold with his father in 1915. Many soldiers returning from World War I came to the area and dug the first underground residences.
20 A settlement took shape, which Aborigines (the original inhabitants of the area) called *Kupa Piti*, meaning "White Man's Burrow."

Most miners arrived in the 1960s and 1970s, **immigrating** to Australia and Coober Pedy
25 from around the globe. The current population of 3,500 includes members of more than 40 **ethnic** or national groups, including Greeks, Poles, Germans, Italians, Serbs, and Croats. They live together in relative harmony,
30 producing 80 percent of the world's opals. Dealers from Hong Kong buy the opals directly from the miners because large companies cannot mine here. Mining permits are sold only to individuals or small groups.

ROUGH EDGES

35 Like many mining communities, Coober Pedy is a rough and rugged town. Trucks with "Explosives" signs on their sides clatter[2] around the streets. A sign outside the drive-in movie theater politely asks patrons not to
40 bring in any dynamite. The miners may enjoy a rough kind of fun—including occasional fights—but the community takes a **liberal** attitude toward this behavior.

A dug-out home

---
[1] *subterranean:* underground, from the Latin sub, meaning "under," and terra, meaning "land"
[2] *clatter:* make noise, such as when metal pieces repeatedly hit each other

Its rough edges **notwithstanding**, Coober Pedy
has a warmth and raw charm. Many residents
claim that long ago they stopped off only for
gasoline and never left. Some fell in love with the
unique (though sometimes scary) scenery. Just
outside town are colorful rocky areas, used as the
location for numerous films, including *Red Planet*
and *Mad Max Beyond Thunderdome*. All around,
the dry land forms a moonscape[3] cut through by
fencing, which keeps wild dogs out of the sheep-
farming country to the south and east.

Tourism is flourishing, and unlucky miners have
opened opal shops, cafés, and underground
motels. Still, this is a working town, and tourists
had better watch their step. Peter Rowe, formerly
the head of the Mine Rescue Squad, pulled plenty
of badly injured people out of mine shafts[4] during
his career. The dirt tracks that cross the opal
fields have many signs warning walkers to watch
their step. Tourists have died after carelessly
walking backwards while taking photographs.

HOME IS WHERE THE DIRT IS

To **create** a typical dug-out, you need a hill and a
drill. Most home-diggers tunnel into a hillside,
which is a lot easier than digging straight down. If
the hill doesn't have a side of exposed rock,
bulldozers push sand and loose soil away until a
sandstone face **emerges**. Dug-outs in the 1980s,
before Coober Pedy established a town
government, were usually blasted into a hillside,
not actually dug. Drilling, with huge machines
meant to dig tunnels through mountains, is now
the **technique** of choice.

The homes are essentially artificial caves, but
don't **assume** there is anything primitive about
them. Three-bedroom plans are common, and
having your cave drilled out costs about the same
as building a new above-ground home of **similar**
size. Needless to say, the **structure** is solid,

[3] *moonscape:* a view of the surface of the moon
[4] *shaft:* vertical tunnel or deep hole

which **creates** some challenges. Electrical
wiring has to be placed in grooves in the rock
and then plastered over. Plumbing is set in
similar grooves.

Interior of a dug-out home

The hills inside the town limits were all
claimed soon after the comforts of dug-out
living became well known. Coober Pedy had to
expand, not because it needed more space
but because it needed more hills. Some town
planners **predict** that Coober Pedy will sprawl
out to great distances as more miners seek a
place to dig. Some paved roads have been
laid, most of them running along the faces of
the hills and out to mine shafts. A lot more
will be needed if homeowners head to the
faraway hills.

One comfortable dug-out illustrates the
advantages of underground living. Outside, it
is pushing 104° Fahrenheit (40° Celsius). This
is relatively mild for January in Coober Pedy,
but hot nonetheless. Inside, it is wonderfully
cool. The low ceiling and honey-colored stone
walls give a feeling of safety and refuge. Area
rugs and comfortable furniture soften the
interior. Appliances are set into custom-
carved spaces. Hole sweet hole.

Reading Comprehension

Mark each sentence as *T* (true) or *F* (false) according to the information in Reading 1. Use the dictionary to help you understand new words.

___ 1. Underground homes are considered normal in Coober Pedy.

___ 2. The first underground homes in Coober Pedy were built by Aborigines.

___ 3. All the opals located in and near Coober Pedy belong to one trading company.

___ 4. Coober Pedy has liberal attitudes toward miners' behavior.

___ 5. The environment around Coober Pedy is dry and rocky.

___ 6. Some tourists have died from falling into holes in the town.

___ 7. Most underground structures in Coober Pedy were originally opal mines.

___ 8. The cost of creating an underground home is similar to the cost of building a home on the surface.

___ 9. It is easier to dig an underground home into a hillside than into the ground.

___10. So far, only one underground home in Coober Pedy has water service.

Vocabulary Activities | STEP I: Word Level

A. Read these excerpts from another article on underground homes. For each excerpt, cross out the one word or phrase in parentheses with a different meaning from the other three choices. Compare answers with a partner.

1. Unlike most homes, underground homes can be (*located / built / structured / positioned*) on steep surfaces. They take up very little surface space.

2. Underground building (*methods / houses / techniques / processes*) mostly use materials already available at the home site.

3. A typical above-ground house makes (*careful / heavy / extensive / liberal*) use of energy, mostly for heating and cooling. An underground home needs little or no heating or cooling, because underground temperatures remain stable. Consequently, it uses only about 20% of the energy used in a conventional home.

4. Underground (*environments / settings / surroundings / creations*) provide excellent noise insulation. Underground homes are exceptionally quiet places to live.

5. Finally, underground houses have a (*special / well-known / unique / one-of-a-kind*) ability to blend in with nature. This not only looks nice but also preserves habitat for wildlife.

The word *notwithstanding* means "not being prevented by." It can come before a noun or noun phrase (*Notwithstanding* the rain, the players finished the game) or after one (The rain *notwithstanding*, the players finished the game).

CORPUS

B. Read each pair of sentences. Check (✓) the ones that can be made into one sentence using *notwithstanding*, and then write the sentences in your notebook. Compare answers in a small group. Discuss what connectors (*because*, *therefore*, *yet*, etc.) you could use for the other sentences.

✓ 1. Daytime temperatures can be extreme. Some people still walk around above ground.

   *The extreme daytime heat **nothwithstanding**, some people still walk around above ground.*

___ 2. Coober Pedy is known for its uncomfortable heat and dryness. People like living there.

___ 3. Building a dug-out is a great challenge. More and more miners want underground homes.

___ 4. A system of roads out to the hills is under development. Many people are planning to build underground homes there.

___ 5. Tourism is flourishing in Coober Pedy. There are many shops, cafés, and motels.

___ 6. Tourists sometimes have accidents in Coober Pedy. Signs tell them to be careful.

___ 7. The people of Coober Pedy come from more than 40 ethnic groups. They work together very well.

Vocabulary Activities STEP II: Sentence Level

Word Form Chart			
Noun	**Verb**	**Adjective**	**Adverb**
prediction	predict	predictable predicted	predictably

To *predict* something means "to say something is likely to happen in the future."

   *Town planners **predict** that in the next few years, more people will want underground homes.*

Predict is also often used to talk about weather.

   *Forecasters are **predicting** another hot day tomorrow.*

CORPUS

C. Answer these questions in your notebook. Use the form of *predict* in parentheses. Compare sentences with a partner. Refer to Reading 1 for information.

1. You want to buy 100 opals. What can you guess about their origins? (*predict*)

   *I can **predict** that about 80 of them will be from Coober Pedy.*

2. Why do people in Coober Pedy not get upset about fights and other rough behavior? (*predictable*)

3. What would the weather service normally say about tomorrow's weather in Coober Pedy? (*predict*)

4. Someone is planning to construct an underground home in Coober Pedy. What tools will he or she probably use? (*prediction*)

5. Imagine that people do not build a large number of homes in the hills far from town. In that case, what could you say about the development of Coober Pedy's road system? (*predicted*)

Word Form Chart			
Noun	**Verb**	**Adjective**	**Adverb**
assumption	assume	assumed	_____
creation creator creativity	create	creative	creatively
emergence	emerge	emergent	_____
similarity	_____	similar	similarly
structure	structure	structural	structurally

D. Read these sentences about underground structures. Then restate each of the sentences in your notebook, using the words in parentheses. Do not change the meanings of the sentences. Be prepared to read aloud or discuss your sentences in class.

1. Underground homes may or may not be safe. Anyone who is planning to live in one should check it carefully. (*assume*)

   *Anyone planning to live in an underground home should not just **assume** it is safe but should check it carefully.*

2. The roof of a dug-out could collapse if there are not enough walls in the underground space to support it. (*structure, structural,* or *structurally*)

3. A harmful gas called radon is naturally present in most soil, and it slowly makes its way into underground spaces. (*emergence* or *emerge*)

4. Since rainwater naturally flows downward from the ground, people who live underground have to expect water problems. (*assumption* or *assume*)

5. When designing an air-circulation system for a home underground, a builder has to think flexibly and imaginatively. (*creative*)

6. Too much moisture and not enough fresh air can make an underground home moldy, like a pile of wet clothes. (*similarly* or *similar*)

Before You Read

Read these questions. Discuss your answers in a small group.

1. Have you ever been in a tunnel, an underpass, a cave, or some other space underground? Was it uncomfortable or frightening? Why or why not?

2. If you dug a hole in your neighborhood, what do you think you would find at various depths: 6 inches (about 15 centimeters), 2 feet (about 0.6 meter), 10 feet (about 3 meters), and 50 feet (about 15 meters)?

3. Why do cities put water pipes, gas pipes, electric lines, and other utility equipment underground instead of aboveground?

READING SKILL | Previewing and Predicting

APPLY

Preview the reading by looking at the title, headings, and photos. Based on your preview, what do you think the reading is about? Write your prediction(s). Then compare them with a partner.

_____

_____

_____

Read

This article from a local magazine in Philadelphia, Pennsylvania (Philly), examines the underground systems on which the city depends.

Understanding Philly's Basement

Philadelphia, a large city on the east coast of the United States, is one of the oldest and most important cities in the country. People walking through the city **assume** they
5 are standing on a rock-solid place. In reality, just below the surface is a vast, dark, and complex **environment**—water pipes, sewers, electrical wires, and television cables. There are also tunnels, abandoned subway stations,
10 graves, hidden waterways, archaeological sites, mines, and more.

Sometimes, one of these underground **structures** fails. A small break in a pipe can eventually **create** a sinkhole that swallows
15 whatever stood above it. One June day, in a **location** not far from Philly, two cars fell 70 feet

when an enormous sinkhole opened up in a busy highway. That same day, two truckers were killed after their rigs fell into a sinkhole on Interstate 99 in New York State, to the north of Pennsylvania.

AN UNDERGROUND MYSTERY

So just how bad are things down there in lower Philadelphia? The answer is simple and frightening: We don't know.

Philadelphia was carefully planned out by William Penn, who established the city in 1682. The well-organized Mr. Penn obviously had little influence below the surface. The city's underground has been built, **liberally** expanded, and repaired in no particular order for more than 300 years. Some underground work was never documented. For example, in the mid-1800s, anti-slavery groups hid escaped slaves in secret shelters below ground to keep them from being kidnapped and returned to the South. In the past, various **ethnic** groups in the city were sometimes fearful or suspicious of city authorities. They built underground meeting rooms, storehouses, and even treasure vaults for their communities.

A car falls into a sinkhole

Even if records were kept, they may be of no help. Many have been scattered or lost, or were simply inaccurate to begin with. This matters for many reasons. The most important is that new systems are hard to plan unless you know where the old ones are. And then there are sinkholes. Until we figure out exactly what is where, we cannot **predict** where the next man-eating hole might develop.

MAPPING THE DEPTHS

"Philadelphia is an old city," says Lucio Soibelman, an associate professor of civil and **environmental** engineering at Carnegie Mellon University, "so you have old infrastructure[1] and new infrastructure. You have new pipes that are being mapped with GIS (geographic information systems) technology and you have old things that no one knows are there. This is not something that was designed in a perfect way. There's a lot going on, and a lot of research is needed to find out what is underground."

The most common **technique** for finding buried pipes or cables is to use a kind of metal detector. The problem is that many underground utilities aren't metal. Many gas pipes are plastic. The channels of the sewer system are lined with baked clay or plastic. To make it easier for people to find them again, most glass fiber optic cables and many newer nonmetallic pipes contain "tracer wires" that can be picked up by metal detectors. Older pipes, however, remain invisible.

Ground penetrating radar (GPR) is an important new tool. In a way, it is **similar** to the sonar systems used to **locate** objects under water. GPR sends thousands of radar pulses per second into the ground. The signals are then either absorbed or reflected back to a receiver. Software senses how long it takes the GPR signals to bounce back. Differences of even a nanosecond in bounce-back time will be registered. A software-generated image of what lies beneath the surface soon **emerges** on the receiver's screen.

---

[1] infrastructure: the basic **structures** and systems of a city or country, such as roads, sewers, etc.

An underground mystery **unique** to Philadelphia was finally unraveled in 2005 by using GPR. An escape tunnel under Eastern State Penitentiary (a prison) in the Fairmount neighborhood was used in 1945 by a group of twelve prisoners. Their clever tunneling work **notwithstanding,** they were all easily recaptured in the city. Their muddy footprints showed exactly where they were hiding. Authorities knew where the tunnel started, but they didn't know until the 2005 GPR readings exactly where it went. The detection of other abandoned tunnels is important to law-enforcement authorities. Such underground passageways could be used by persons trying to **immigrate** illegally through Philly's seaport. Smugglers[2] or other criminals could also find them useful. The police want to know where they are, and GPR is a big help.

Robots that can patrol large water systems are another great innovation. They are already used in other cities. In Pittsburgh, for example, a robotic system called Responder travels inside sewers, operated by a remote control, looking for problems in the pipes. Responder is equipped with laser and sonar sensors that scan the insides of pipe walls. The slightest bit of corrosion[3] or the smallest leak will register. Advanced software can then construct extremely detailed 3-D models of the pipe walls.

OK. NOW WHAT?

Locating problems is important, but it's not enough. Fixing them is the bulk of the job. Fixing and updating underground utilities in a city is very complicated. It's not just a matter of digging a hole, pulling out bad pipes, and installing good ones. The city and its neighborhoods must continue functioning during the many months it takes to put things right.

A company named Insituform has developed technology that can fix a pipe from the inside before it breaks, without any digging. Workers fill a tube with a special kind of resin (a sticky substance) and send it through the pipe. Then they heat the water inside the pipe. The resin expands outward, attaches to the interior surface of the pipe, and then hardens. This **creates** a new pipe inside the old pipe.

The company actually used this **technique** on the sewers under one of the most famous buildings in the United States, the White House, in Washington, D.C. The pipes dated from the mid-1800s and needed extensive repair. For security reasons—and because it would look really ugly—the government decided not to dig up the lawn, but rather to work underground, and under tourists' feet. ■

A tunnel under Philadelphia

[2] *smugglers:* people who takes goods in or out of a place illegally and in secret
[3] *corrosion:* weakening or breaking apart because of the action of a chemical

Reading Comprehension

Mark each sentence as *T* (true) or *F* (false) according to the information in Reading 2.
Use the dictionary to help you understand new words.

— 1. Philadelphia no longer locates pipes or cables underground.

— 2. The collapse of underground structures sometimes kills people traveling on
the surface.

— 3. William Penn carefully planned Philadelphia's underground environment in
the 1680s.

— 4. Some residents of Philadelphia today use underground structures to hide
things from city officials.

— 5. Old infrastructure is easier to locate than new infrastructure.

— 6. GPR can detect even non-metal items.

— 7. By using GPR, the police easily recaptured twelve escaped prisoners.

— 8. Systems like Responder use radar or sonar to find out where old sewers are.

— 9. Robots can discover problems by looking at pipes from the inside.

—10. The sewers under the White House were fixed by creating new pipes inside
old ones.

Vocabulary Activities STEP I: Word Level

A. Underground exploring (UE) involves traveling through tunnels and other hidden
parts of a city. Complete the sentences about UE using the target vocabulary in
the box. Use the synonyms in parentheses to help you. (Note: The sentences are
not in order.)

assume	environment	notwithstanding	unique
emerge	liberal	similar to	

a. Perhaps because people are fascinated by hidden things, underground spaces

have always had a _____ appeal to explorers.
(not found anywhere else)

b. Police often arrest UE groups as they _____ from tunnels and
(come out)

charge them with trespassing.

c. Urban explorers generally take a very _____ approach
(unrestricted)

to property rights. As long as they aren't damaging anything, they

_____ they have the right to use the property.
(believe)

d. MIT was only one of several hot spots for UEs. Informal groups

_____ the MIT group explored the undergrounds of Paris,
(like)

Toronto, and Sydney.

e. Starting in the 1970s, a movement called "urban exploration" (UE) took special notice of rarely visited parts of the underground _____ (space) , like tunnels, drains, and abandoned subway stations.

f. Students at the Massachusetts Institute of Technology (MIT) contributed greatly to the UE culture. _____ (despite) the fact that it was illegal, they developed a tradition of exploring the steam tunnels at the university.

B. Tell the story of urban exploration by putting the sentences in activity A in order from first (1) to last (6). More than one order may be possible. Then use the target words as you compare stories with a partner.

1. _a_
2. ___
3. ___
4. ___
5. ___
6. ___

Many English words have several related meanings. *Locate* is an example. All its meanings refer to "place," but in slightly different ways. A good dictionary will list these meanings for *locate* and its related forms.

CORPUS

C. Look up *locate* and its forms in your dictionary. Then read these sample sentences and answer the questions that follow. Compare answers with a partner.

a. On my first day in the new office, I tried to **locate** all the fire exits on my floor.

b. After looking at several cities, Caitlin decided to **relocate** to Chicago.

c. To ensure privacy, it is best to **locate** trees and bushes between your house and your neighbor's house.

d. The university has a beautiful **location** on the shores of Lake Martin.

1. Check (✓) the word closest in meaning to *locate*. Look up each choice in your dictionary before you answer.

   ___ situate

   ___ move

   ___ inhabit

   ___ clear

2. Sentences a, b, and c in the box above show three slightly different meanings of the verb *locate* and forms related to it. Write the letter of the sentence next to the correct meaning.

   ___ to set up a home or business in a new place

   ___ to search for and find something

   ___ to put something into a place

3. Look at the sample sentences in your dictionary for *locate* and its forms. What is being located in each of those samples?

   _____

   _____

   _____

   _____

4. Check (✓) next to each real meaning of *location*. (Not every item should be checked.) Confirm your choices with your dictionary.

   ___ moving from one place to another

   ___ a place where a movie is filmed

   ___ finding where something is

   ___ a point of view on a political issue

   ___ a site

To *assume* something is to believe it without checking whether it is true. Our assumptions are reflected in what we do and how we see the world. For example, you probably assume that a person wearing a police uniform is a police officer.

CORPUS

D. In each of these situations, at least one assumption lies behind the action. Write one assumption for each action in the right column. Be ready to discuss your answers with a partner.

Action	Assumption
A customer goes to a bank and gives a teller several thousand dollars to deposit.	
A student tells her deepest thoughts and secrets to her best friend.	
A football player walks alone at night through a very rough part of town.	
On the highway, someone drives at speeds slightly over the speed limit.	

E. Incorrect assumptions can be embarrassing or even dangerous. Rank these (possibly) incorrect assumptions from *1* (most dangerous) to *6* (least dangerous).

___ If someone mentions a doctor, he or she is referring to a man, not a woman.

___ A manager always does what is best for the company's employees.

___ It doesn't matter what your grades are, as long as you finish school.

___ The groceries I buy have been officially inspected, so they're safe.

___ If I tell someone a secret, he or she won't tell it to other people.

___ Car accidents only happen to other people, not to me.

As a class, make a chart and tally everyone's answers. Which assumption does the class consider most dangerous? Least dangerous? Why do you think this is true?

F. Discuss these questions in a small group. Use the dictionary to clarify word meanings, if necessary.

1. In which environment would an underground house be hardest to build? Why?

   a. a tropical rainforest

   b. New York City

   c. Antarctica

   d. a desert

2. Think about a town or city you know well. Which of these structures or services does it have underground? Who owns them? Why were they put underground?

   a. homes

   b. tunnels

   c. sewers

   d. electrical lines

G. Look at these arguments for and against urban exploration. Restate each idea in your notebook, using the word in parentheses. Then write a paragraph that expresses your own opinion. Use as many target words as possible in your work. Be prepared to read aloud or discuss your paragraph in class.

For	Against
Serious urban explorers cause no damage to the structures they explore. Their rule is, "Take only pictures. Leave only footprints." (*assume*)	Not every urban explorer is harmless. Some steal from the places they enter. Others spray graffiti there. (*assume*)
Although some underground spaces are dangerous, urban explorers can prepare themselves well. They are ready for dangers like steam explosions or live electrical wires. (*predict*)	Old tunnels and other underground spaces could contain dozens of dangers, from toxic chemicals to collapsing roofs. No one knows what is there. And explorers can't protect themselves from the most serious ones, like steam explosions. (*predict*)
Any member of the general public has the right to use abandoned property as long as he or she doesn't damage it. (*location*)	Urban explorers do not have any right to enter restricted underground spaces. This is trespassing—being in a place without the permission of its owner— and it is wrong. (*location*)

H. Self-Assessment Review: Go back to page 1 and reassess your knowledge of the target vocabulary. How has your understanding of the words changed? What words do you feel most comfortable with now?

Writing and Discussion Topics

Write about or discuss the following topics.

1. Above-ground houses are attractive for some reasons. Underground houses are attractive for other reasons. Which would you prefer to live in, and why?

2. Much of Reading 2 is about Philadelphia's efforts simply to locate underground systems. If you were planning a new city, what could you do to make sure your city would not face a problem like Philadelphia's? Be specific about the procedures or equipment you would use.

3. Some structures or systems are placed underground for security reasons. For example, an underground water system is less likely to be damaged than one above ground. Describe some ways in which an underground location provides better security than an above-ground location.

UNIT 2

The Business of Branding

In this unit, you will

> read about the branding of products and its importance for business.
> review previewing and predicting.
> increase your understanding of the target academic words for this unit.

READING SKILLS Finding the Main Idea; Finding Details

Self-Assessment

Think about how well you know each target word, and check (✓) the appropriate column. I have…

TARGET WORDS	never seen the word before	seen the word but am not sure what it means	seen the word and understand what it means	used the word, but am not sure if correctly	used the word confidently in *either* speaking *or* writing	used the word confidently in *both* speaking *and* writing
AWL						
consume						
contradict						
🔑 convert						
corporate						
equate						
🔑 finance						
🔑 label						
🔑 medium						
presume						
🔑 register						
revenue						
subsidy						
🔑 symbol						
🔑 theme						

🔑 Oxford 3000™ keywords

Outside the Reading What do you know about branding?
Watch the video on the student website to find out more.

Before You Read

Read these questions. Discuss your answers in a small group.

1. Think about some basic products you buy (toothpaste, soft drinks, etc.). What brands are they? List at least five products for which you usually choose the same brands.

2. Why do people often buy the same brand?

3. In your opinion, what is the highest-quality brand of car in the world? Why do you think so?

MORE WORDS YOU'LL NEED

blog: a Web log, a personal website on which someone expresses opinions or gives personal information

subculture: a set of activities, objects, and beliefs associated with a group within a larger culture

REVIEW A SKILL Previewing and Predicting (See p. 2)

Look at the headings and the pictures in Reading 1. From the headings, which topics do you think the reading will cover? Why do you think the reading has pictures of a car and motorcycles?

Read

This magazine article is about the influence that a brand can have on its customers and their culture.

The Power of Branding

Let's say your company has been making athletic shoes for 50 or 60 years. They are good shoes. Nevertheless, other companies have sped past you in the race for
5 fame and the **revenue** that goes with it. Products with the logos of the other companies are status **symbols**. Products with your logo make people think of basketball stars from the 1980s. To turn things around, you have to **convert** your
10 product's old-fashioned image into something new, and make sure **consumers** get the message. They must **equate** your product with some larger idea that has nothing to do with[1] shoes—beauty, wealth, or even world peace. In
15 other words, you have to build a brand.

FROM THE RANCH TO ROLLS-ROYCE
The term *brand* comes from the practice of using a hot iron to burn a distinctive mark into the skin of a cow or a horse. For example, the owner of the Double Jay Ranch might brand a
20 "JJ" mark on his or her stock. This brand helps the rancher distinguish his or her animals from others. The brand is a kind of **label**, a device for creating recognition. Branding of products is also all about recognition.

25 People **equate** the name *Rolls-Royce*, for example, with classic luxury. The recognition value of this brand is enormous. It even **registers** with people who have never seen one of the company's cars. When the German

---

[1] *has nothing to do with:* is not related to or connected to

company BMW bought the Rolls company in 1998, they were careful to change nothing. They continued to build cars in Greenwood, England, because Rolls-Royce is thought of as British. Not even BMW—a powerful brand itself—has the
35 same aristocratic image. Rolls-Royce turned 100 years old in 2004, and the brand continues to use the **themes** of integrity, dependability, and even Britishness in its advertising.

ROLLS-ROYCE DRIVERS AND NASCAR

As the story of Rolls-Royce shows, an extremely
40 successful brand may become a lasting part of a culture. When that happens to a brand with a worldwide presence, the company may get **contradictory** results. In its home culture, the brand may benefit from being a sort of national
45 treasure; however, it may suffer overseas from being a **symbol** of foreignness. The McDonald's restaurant franchise offers just one prominent case of a **corporation** fighting to guide its brand through these difficult situations.
50   Subcultures can form around a certain brand. NASCAR (the National Association for Stock Car Auto Racing) is in business to organize auto races and sell related products, but its brand is about much more than that.
55 NASCAR was founded in the late 1940s and originally built its image around beachside racing in Daytona, Florida. It revised its brand through the 1980s and 1990s to appeal to a broader audience. Nearly 75 million Americans
60 now consider themselves part of a NASCAR subculture.
      Because NASCAR has a connection to such a large segment of the population, it is a **medium** in itself. It can **finance** many of its operations
65 by, for instance, allowing its name to appear on

products and selling advertising space alongside its racetracks.

MY BRAND, MYSELF

Among some strong brands, the line between promotional and personal image is unclear.
70 Some customers may adopt a brand's image as their own image. The ads for Nike shoes show no-nonsense athletes. A customer might buy Nike shoes because she considers herself a no-nonsense athlete—and she wants others to
75 **presume** this, too.

      Biker subculture in the United States owes a great deal to the branding success of the Harley-Davidson motorcycle company. Its American-manufactured motorbikes are promoted as a
80 **symbol** of patriotism. Harley has also managed to turn its motorcycles into **symbols** of opposition to mainstream[2] cultural values. In a radio interview, Harley-Davidson's CEO, Jim Ziemer, points out one way his brand—
85 and its black-and-orange logo—has become very personal.

> **Interviewer:** When business school students study branding, one of the names that's always at the top of that list is Harley-
> 90 Davidson. I'd like you to tell me, first of all, in your mind, what is it that makes a brand?
> **Ziemer:** A brand is made when a person really feels a connection with that brand. I mean, we've taken it to the ultimate, where a
> 95 lot of our customers have a [Harley-Davidson] tattoo on their body so they really feel very special and connected with the brand.

The origins of branding, the hot irons and the Double Jay, seem not so far away. ■

---

[2] *mainstream:* representing the way most people in a culture think or behave

Reading Comprehension

Mark each sentence as *T* (true) or *F* (false) according to the information in Reading 1.
Use the dictionary to help you understand new words.

___ 1. Branding is the process of equating a product with an idea or image.

___ 2. Ranchers brand animals by burning marks into their skin.

___ 3. Rolls-Royce is no longer a British corporation.

___ 4. The Rolls-Royce brand has lost revenue because it is associated with old things.

___ 5. In many countries, people don't like to buy products with foreign brand names.

___ 6. NASCAR is a political organization that has created a brand.

___ 7. People often presume a person fits the image of a brand because he or she uses the brand's product.

___ 8. Harley-Davidson motorcycles are manufactured outside the United States.

___ 9. The Harley-Davidson brand is associated with classic luxury.

___10. Some people have Harley-Davidson symbols tattooed on their skin.

READING SKILL   Finding the Main Idea

LEARN

The main ideas in Reading 1 appear as "chunks," and the different chunks
are separated by headings. A chunk may consist of one paragraph or several
paragraphs. Recognizing these chunks can help you see relationships between
main ideas and details.

APPLY

Use the list of phrases to identify the main idea of each chunk in Reading 1. Then
circle the paragraph number(s) to indicate which paragraph(s) make up the chunk.

- branding as a tool for recognition
- brands and self-image
- brands as part of culture
- why companies build brands

Chunk 1 _why companies build brands_   (1) 2 3 4 5 6 7 8

Chunk 2 _____   1 2 3 4 5 6 7 8

Chunk 3 _____   1 2 3 4 5 6 7 8

Chunk 4 _____   1 2 3 4 5 6 7 8

A. Read these excerpts from another article about branding. For each excerpt, cross out the one word or phrase in parentheses with a different meaning from the other three choices. Compare answers with a partner.

1. Research has found that the (*symbols / revenues / logos / labels*) of popular brands activate parts of the brain linked to positive emotions.

2. The researchers used fMRI machines (functional Magnetic Resonance Imaging) to monitor brain activity while 20 people looked at the logos for several brands of companies and products. The scientists (*converted / compared / matched / related*) the fMRI data to what neurologists already know about different parts of the brain.

3. They discovered that easily recognized brands caused activity specifically in the areas of the brain that are active when people have positive feelings. The lesser-known brands, however, (*registered with / made an impression on / had an effect on / harmed*) many parts of the brain, including some associated with negative feelings.

4. Many neurologists who have read about the study agree that the brain has to work harder when shown the unfamiliar brands, and this effort is unpleasant. (*Companies / Corporations / Departments / Firms*) can learn a lesson from this: expose people to your brand over and over again, so it becomes familiar.

5. The study also confirms a belief common among both advertisers and neurologists. Good advertising should not necessarily give information. Rather, it should create emotions, so people (*associate / equate / connect / reward*) a brand with feeling good.

As an adjective, the word *medium* refers to anything that is not large and not small, but somewhere between, as in "a person of medium height."

As a noun, however, *medium* has a completely different meaning. It refers to a way to convey or send something. The plural form is *media*.

*Some chemical reactions require a **medium** to help them take place.*

*Television and radio are popular **media** for getting the news.*

CORPUS

B. What is each of these things a medium for? List as many things as you can. Discuss your ideas with a partner.

1. a newspaper: _____

2. the telephone system: _____

3. a letter: _____

4. the postal service: _____

5. the Internet: _____

6. gossip: _____

The verb *subsidize* means "to give money to someone or an organization to help pay for something." The noun is *subsidy*.

*The city **subsidizes** ambulance companies in order to keep the price of their services low.*

*These companies could not continue to operate without **subsidies** from the city.*

CORPUS

C. Read these pairs of items. With a partner, write down some ways that the first item might subsidize the second. Then, in a small group, discuss whether you think the subsidies should exist or should continue. Give reasons for your opinions.

1. parent / child's education: _____

2. government / students: _____

3. government / small businesses: _____

4. employer / employee's healthcare: _____

5. employer / employee's education: _____

6. local government / rent: _____

Word Form Chart			
Noun	**Verb**	**Adjective**	**Adverb**
consumption consumer	consume	consumable	_____
corporation	incorporate	corporate	_____
presumption	presume	presumable presumed	presumably
symbol symbolism	symbolize	symbolic	symbolically
theme	_____	thematic	thematically

D. Read these excerpts from an article about branding. Then restate the essential information in your notebook, using the words in parentheses. Focus on main ideas and leave out unnecessary details. Be prepared to read aloud or discuss your sentences in class.

1. Your first big decision should be: How will you get your brand out to the public? (*consumer*)

   The first thing you have to decide is how to let possible **consumers** *know about your brand.*

2. If you decide to advertise, first decide what role the ads will play in your business development plan. (*corporate*)

3. What idea do you want your products to represent? How will they represent it? (*symbolize*)

4. Is your goal in advertising to promote name awareness? One way is to use memorable images that are not specifically related to your product. One insurance company in the United States, AFLAC, used a duck in many of their ads. The duck quacked "AFLAC" in different situations where a person might need insurance. At the time, 90% of Americans recognized the company's name. (*theme*)

5. Test your ad ideas before you spend money on them. Teens are especially hard to target. They go through images in a few weeks and go on looking for the next new thing. (*consume*)

6. To illustrate this point, a government agency once spent $929 million on an anti-drug campaign targeted at teens. They thought the ads would be very powerful, but they didn't test them on teens. After the ads started running, they discovered that kids ignored them. (*presumed*)

Some verbs *collocate* with, or often occur with, certain prepositions. These sets of words are called *collocations*. Here are some examples of collocations for target words in this unit:

convert to/into	*A transformer **converts** one type of electric current <u>into</u> another.*
equate with	*Teenagers often **equate** unusual clothes <u>with</u> personal freedom.*
register with	*I don't like this ad. The images just don't **register** <u>with</u> me.*
finance by/with	*Youth sports programs **finance** their activities <u>by</u> selling tickets.*
	*They **finance** their activities <u>with</u> the revenue from ticket sales.*

CORPUS

E. Answer these questions using the verb in parentheses. Be sure to use a preposition that collocates with it. Refer to the chart above and Reading 1 for information. Compare answers with a partner.

1. Why are symbols like the Rolls-Royce badge or the Harley-Davidson logo so powerful? (*register*)

   _____

   _____

2. Why does a weak brand harm the sales of a product? (*equate*)

   _____

   _____

3. How do the license fees for NASCAR's name help the organization? (*finance*)

   _____

   _____

4. Why would a stronger brand help the shoe company mentioned in Paragraph 1 of the reading? (*convert*)

   _____

   _____

Before You Read

Read these questions. Discuss your answers in a small group.

1. When you are watching TV and an advertisement comes on, what do you do? Do you watch it, or do you do something else?

2. Name two or three movies that you really like. Think of some products that the characters use—cars, clothing, food, etc. Can you recall the brands of any of these products?

3. Are you more likely to buy a product if you see it being used in a TV show, a movie, a video game, or some other form of entertainment? Why or why not?

REVIEW A SKILL Previewing and Predicting (See p. 2)

Look at the headings and the pictures in Reading 2. From the headings, which topics do you think the reading will cover? The picture of cartoon characters is from a TV show, and the picture of the car is from a movie. Why do you think they are in a reading titled "Product Placement"?

Read

This magazine article looks at the way advertisers get their products into TV shows, movies, and other forms of entertainment.

PRODUCT PLACEMENT

The Japanese television series *Tiger and Bunny* started in 2011 as an advertiser's dream. Cartoon superheroes do good deeds partly so they can wear costumes with
5 company names on them. A character named Wild Tiger wears a suit bearing the names of S.H. Figuarts (a Japanese toy company) and a **media** company named SoftBank. Other characters wear suits with **labels** for
10 the Bandai game company, Pepsi soft drinks, and the food company Calbee. Each **corporate** sponsor of the show is assigned to one of the heroes. No sponsor is linked with any bad guy, because that would **contradict** the
15 branding message.

The sponsors of *Tiger and Bunny* depend not on commercial breaks but on product placement— inserting products into the show's plot[1] and setting. A brand is the set of
20 images that arise when the name of a company or product is mentioned. In *Tiger and Bunny*, a company name **symbolizes** the doing of good deeds, and this builds a great brand image. The sponsors believe that they can
25 generate **revenue** by linking their brands to likeable characters. For TV networks and movie companies, product placement is great because it costs very little while earning significant income to help **subsidize** their
30 shows and films.

---
[1] *plot:* the story in a TV show, movie, book, etc.

THE IMPORTANCE OF PLACEMENT

Product placement can take many forms. In *Tiger and Bunny*, it is readily apparent. In other cases, it is more subtle. The product doesn't even have to fit the **theme** of the show. A movie
35 or TV character might check email on an Apple computer and then sit at a breakfast table with a box of Kellogg's Corn Flakes. He gets into his car, a Honda, and then answers his Nokia cell phone. Each product is part of the background,
40 not a featured part of the movie. In the viewer's mind, the product **registers** as the normal thing to use.

Companies may turn to product placement to reach **consumers** at unusual times. A business
45 cannot stop a movie at a theater to show commercials. To a company, this is a wasted opportunity. Hundreds of potential customers are sitting together, all their eyes focused on a screen for nearly two hours, and no one is thinking about
50 the company's products. How can the company **convert** that film into a **medium** that carries product messages? The logical way is to put a soft drink, or car, or refrigerator into the movie. If the film is good, viewers will **equate** its high
55 quality with that of the product.

In any case, viewers are unlikely to shut a placed product out of their consciousness. This helps solve a longstanding problem for advertisers—getting **consumers** to watch. Since the early days
60 of television, viewers have walked away from their TVs during commercials, and newer technologies have made ad-skipping even easier. With digital video recorders (DVRs), people can record TV shows to watch later and can fast-forward through
65 the commercials. A survey in 2010 found that 53% of households in the United States with DVRs really do skip commercials. Many viewers now watch TV on their smartphones, which have a lot of "distraction **media**" like music and games.
70 One study showed that when a commercial came on, 73% of people watching the show online switched to some form of distraction **media.**

AN EFFECTIVE STRATEGY

Showcasing products is not free. In 2009, spending on product placement was $6.25 billion
75 worldwide. More than half of that—$3.7 billion—was by U.S. companies. **Financing** product placement may be a better use of money than buying ordinary advertising. The average cost of a 30-second commercial on a U.S.
80 TV network is $175,000, so 10 minutes of exposure for a product would cost $3.5 million. For that amount of money, a product could get placement in an average TV show for three or four years.

The yellow Camaro featured in the 2007 movie *Tranformers*

85 Evidence suggests that product placement can really work. The first *Transformers* movie (2007), about robots that could change into cars and trucks, featured a yellow sports car called the Camaro. Sales of Camaros had
90 fallen off, and the Chevrolet car brand was not sure whether to keep producing them. Then came the *Transformers* movie. David Caldwell, an official at Chevrolet, says that Camaro sales have been increasing since the
95 movie came out, and 10% of buyers have purchased yellow ones. Product placers, however, should not **presume** that viewers will always react positively. In Australia, the first season of a TV series called *The Block* helped
100 increase the sales of Black & Decker tools, which are often used in the series. However, the second season had too much placement. It lost many viewers who then perceived the show as just one long commercial.

TARGETS IN NEW MEDIA

105 Product-placers have to adapt to new **media,** and many companies have placed products in video games. For example, in the game *Super Monkey Ball* by Sega, every banana has a Dole company sticker on it. Finding the right
110 **medium,** however, is hard. Online videos often

include placements, but most videos have short lifespans. Even if a video goes viral[2], it will probably be mostly forgotten within three or four weeks. Furthermore, a product placement online could expose your company to ridicule[3], because Internet videos are often copied and changed to create joke videos. That is not at all helpful in your efforts to build a brand.

Still, the future of product placement, even online, is bright. Companies may eventually collect enough data about individual Internet users to target them with product-filled content that fits their tastes. If you like boats, your online weather report might show a boat in the background while a friend of yours sees a hotel with the same report. The best an advertiser can hope for is that people walking away from a movie or TV show have discussions about a character's clothing, cars, or furniture as much as about the story itself. Conversations like this about video games, smartphone applications, and popular websites are the next great advertiser's dream.

[2] *goes viral:* spreads very fast online
[3] *ridicule:* make unkind jokes about someone or something

Reading Comprehension

Mark each sentence as *T* (true) or *F* (false) according to the information in Reading 2. Use the dictionary to help you understand new words.

___ 1. Characters in *Tiger and Bunny* wear clothes with company names on them.

___ 2. S.H. Figuarts and SoftBank are characters in the *Tiger and Bunny* show.

___ 3. Product placement occurs mostly during commercial breaks in a TV show.

___ 4. DVRs are a problem for advertisers because they let viewers skip commercials.

___ 5. Products are often placed in the background of a show.

___ 6. Producers of shows pay companies for the right to place their products.

___ 7. Spending on product placement in the U.S. is about five times higher than spending worldwide.

___ 8. The first *Transformers* movie included a yellow Camaro car.

___ 9. Placing products in video games is dangerous because someone could make your product's image into a joke.

___10. Internet marketers may soon know enough about your tastes to place the things you like in content on the Internet.

LEARN

In most pieces of writing, specific facts, processes, and other small points support the main ideas. To understand the author's claims, decide which details match with which main ideas.

APPLY

Read the details from Reading 2 in the box. Write each detail under the main idea that it is related to in the reading. Look back at Reading 2 if necessary. Discuss answers with a partner.

30-second commercial	Camaros	fast-forwarding
$3.7 billion	distraction media	DVRs less of a threat
Wild Tiger	links to superheroes	promotion during a movie
less than one fifth of the U.S. amount	walking away during commercials	associating brands with good guys

examples of product placement

Wild Tiger

_____

_____

problems advertisers have

_____

_____

_____

the cost of product placement

_____

_____

_____

advantages of product placement

_____

_____

_____

A. Complete the sentences about Pokémon products by using the target vocabulary in the box. Use each item one time. Use the synonyms in parentheses to help you.

consumer	equates	presumed	symbols
contradicts	media	registers with	themes
convert			

1. A fad is anything—usually a product or a behavior—that _____ (gets the attention of) the public very strongly, but for only a short time.

2. Clever branding practices can intentionally _____ (turn) an ordinary product into a fad.

3. One of the biggest fads of all time, Pokémon, originated with a Japanese video-game designer who used to collect insects when he was a child. When he created Pokémon, Satoshi Tajiri drew on _____ (recurring ideas) familiar to insect collectors.

4. Most of all, a collector like Tajiri _____ (thinks they are the same) the size of a collection with its quality. The more varieties in your collection, the better it is.

5. Pokémon first appeared in Japanese video games in 1996 and quickly branched off into other _____ (information channels) , from films to books. Pokémon card games were a huge fad in the United States in the late 1990s and early 2000s.

6. The Pokémon brand was strengthened by its presence in these many forms. It also grew because Pokémon's marketers _____ (had a basic belief) that buyers would be like insect collectors, wanting to get bigger and bigger collections. One of Pokémon's slogans in North America was, "Gotta catch 'em all."

7. The basic idea of Pokémon is that a person can capture a number of "pocket monsters," fictional animals with certain powers and abilities. The appearance of a Pokémon may involve _____ (signs) of its abilities. For example, the Pokémon known as Pikachu, which can generate electricity, has a tail that looks like a lightning bolt.

8. The original Pokémon fad had faded by 2004. However, in a situation that _____ (opposes) the normal expectations of a fad's short lifespan, the 649 kinds of Pokémon became popular again in 2011. A new Pokémon movie came out that year, and a new generation of kids began trying to catch 'em all.

B. Read the sample sentences that feature forms of the word *convert*. Then answer the questions that follow. Use your dictionary as suggested in the directions. Compare answers with a partner.

> a. In a process called friction, mechanical energy is **converted** into heat energy.
> b. The Environmental Coalition supports the **conversion** of old coal-burning power plants into modern plants.
> c. At first Professor Davis opposed the new transportation system, but he became a **convert** when he realized how convenient it was.
> d. If you attach a set of wheels to the blade, this ice skate is **convertible** into a roller skate.

1. In the sample sentences in the box, what is converted in each case? What is it converted into?

   a. _____ into _____

   b. _____ into _____

   c. _____ into _____

   d. _____ into _____

2. Look at the sample sentences in your dictionary for *convert* and its forms. What is being converted in each of those samples? What is it converted into?

   _____

   _____

   _____

3. Does *convert* have any forms that are not used in the sample sentences in the box above? If so, what are they? Consult your dictionary.

   _____

Vocabulary Activities STEP II: Sentence Level

Word Form Chart			
Noun	**Verb**	**Adjective**	**Adverb**
contradiction	contradict	contradictory contradicting	_____

C. Answer these questions in your notebook, using the forms of *contradict* in parentheses. Use each form of the word at least once. Refer to Reading 2 for information. Discuss your answers in a small group.

1. Why don't the producers of *Tiger and Bunny* link corporate sponsors to bad guys in the show? (*contradict*)

2. Why does the author of Reading 2 mention product placement in an Australian TV show called *The Block*? (*contradict* or *contradiction*)

3. Some people believe that product placement is not an effective strategy. They think it's entertaining but doesn't really improve sales. How would you argue against this position? Use information from Reading 2. (*contradict* or *contradictory*)

4. Imagine that your company has placed a product in an online video, and someone has stolen it and turned it into a joke video. Why would this be bad for your brand? (*contradiction* or *contradictory*)

D. Imagine that a financial institution is trying to find images that might help it build its brand. Which symbols would be most likely to register with potential clients? Rank them from *1* (most appealing) to *6* (least appealing).

___ a field of spring flowers in the sunshine

___ big buildings in a city center

___ a strong mother or father protecting a family

___ a large ship sailing calmly on rough waters

___ a fortress or castle

___ a young couple, smiling and relaxed

As a class, make a chart on the board and tally everyone's answers. Write a summary of the results using some of the target vocabulary from this unit. Include answers to these questions: Which symbol does your class think is the most effective for a bank to use? Least effective? Why?

E. Look at these arguments for and against common branding practices. Restate each idea in your notebook, using some form of the word in parentheses. Then write a paragraph that expresses your own opinion. Try to use as many target words as possible. Be prepared to discuss your paragraph or debate the issue in class.

For	Against
People shouldn't think that branding is something new. Even in ancient Rome, businesses had slogans. (*presume*)	The use of branding in modern life is huge. The number of channels for advertising and image-building has multiplied many times since home computers became common. (*medium*)
People are eager to buy an image along with a product. Branding satisfies a need for belonging and self-definition. (*consume*)	For some people, brand images register too strongly. They have a hard time separating their own personalities from the image a product presents. (*equate*)
Businesses operate in a crowded marketplace. They have to find a way to distinguish their products from competing products. (*corporate*)	Products should distinguish themselves by quality, value for money, or other traits that are really part of the product. Using brand images to entertain and distract people from these product-related qualities is dishonest. (*theme*)

F. Self-Assessment Review: Go back to page 17 and reassess your knowledge of the target vocabulary. How has your understanding of the words changed? What words do you feel most comfortable with now?

Writing and Discussion Topics

Write about or discuss the following topics.

1. Reading 2 is about product placement. Some people criticize producers of TV shows or movies for letting products into stories. These critics say product placement is dishonest because it promotes products without warning viewers that the promotion is coming. They also say it takes away from the artistic presentation of the story. Do you think these critics are correct or not? Explain your answer.

2. The costs of branding are passed on to consumers. Companies pay for their ads and creative teams by raising prices or reducing services. Do you think this trade-off is good for consumers? Does the brand image associated with a product justify this extra expense?

3. On social-networking websites, like Facebook, users promise not to use the sites to promote products. In reality, though, users recommend their favorite bands, their favorite books, and so on. Brand developers have found ways to advertise without actually advertising. And they benefit from being attached to websites that feel comfortable and personal to their users. Do you think people who promote products should be banned from the websites for breaking the rules? Or is it unavoidable that advertising will leak onto these sites?

UNIT 3

Who Are You, Really?

In this unit, you will

> read about personal-identification technology and how its use affects societies.
> review finding the main idea.
> increase your understanding of the target academic words for this unit.

READING SKILL Scanning

Self-Assessment

Think about how well you know each target word, and check (✓) the appropriate column. I have...

TARGET WORDS	never seen the word before	seen the word but am not sure what it means	seen the word and understand what it means	used the word, but am not sure if correctly	used the word confidently in *either* speaking *or* writing	used the word confidently in *both* speaking *and* writing
AWL						
adjacent						
🔑 analyze						
🔑 anticipate						
consequent						
controversy						
🔑 data						
🔑 device						
equip						
🔑 federal						
🔑 involve						
🔑 justify						
🔑 legal						
modify						
🔑 monitor						
undertake						

🔑 Oxford 3000™ keywords

Outside the Reading What do you know about technology?
Watch the video on the student website to find out more.

Before You Read

Read these questions. Discuss your answers in a small group.

1. Imagine that someone has taken your picture without asking you. How would you feel? Explain why.

2. Police officers have difficulty spotting trouble in large crowds of people. How could technology help the police?

3. Have you ever seen a security camera? Where? Why do you think a camera was placed there?

MORE WORDS YOU'LL NEED

database: a set of information stored in a computer
threat: something that could cause harm

Read

This magazine article is about face-recognition technology used for security at sporting events. It focuses on the technology used at the 2001 Super Bowl—the American football championship game—held in Tampa, Florida.

Looking for Bad Guys at the Big Game

When the Super Bowl came to Tampa, Florida, in 2001, football players and coaches were not the only people on camera. Every fan was of interest to security
5 officials, who used tiny, hard-to-see cameras to capture a shot of each person who passed through the stadium gates.

The organizers of any huge sporting event have to **anticipate** trouble and try to stop it
10 before it starts. Security officials at Tampa's Raymond James Stadium hoped to do so by using machines that recognize faces. Each face seen by the gate-mounted cameras was compared to the **data** in local and **federal**
15 law-enforcement computer systems. The **data** included photos of people previously arrested for stealing, causing fights, and other **illegal** activities. A similar set of automatic eyes routinely surveys the crowds at the Maine Road
20 Ground in Manchester, England, the home stadium for the Manchester City soccer team. If a fan's picture matches one in the database,

security officials could closely **monitor** him or her and perhaps even make an arrest.

A crowd at a sporting event, as viewed through overhead security cameras

INVASION OF PRIVACY?

25 Not everyone thinks this kind of surveillance is a good thing. In the United States, it has stirred some **controversy** about possible threats to the privacy rights of individuals. People being

captured on camera were not
30 told their pictures were being
taken. None of them gave
permission. The technology has
not been proven to be reliable.
What if the system points out an
35 innocent person as a criminal by
mistake? At a very basic level, it
simply makes many people
angry to think of a society in
which the authorities spy on
40 people wherever they go.

Security officials say the
face-recognition (FR) system's
great benefits **justify** any small
inconvenience. Banks, shopping
45 malls, and government buildings
are already **equipped** with
security cameras, and no one has a problem
with that. Why complain about the systems
used at Raymond James Stadium and the Maine
50 Road Ground?

BIOMETRICS

One big difference is that a system like the one
used at the Super Bowl **involves** "biometric"
technology. It **analyzes** facial characteristics
(the features of the face) to establish a person's
55 identity. A biometric system **undertakes** not just
to display or record an event but to instantly
identify the people **involved** in it.

The difference in types of systems is
illustrated by another camera system in Tampa,
60 this one in Ybor City, an entertainment district
adjacent to downtown Tampa. At first, cameras
mounted on the district's utility poles **monitored**
the streets for fights, drug deals, and other
crimes. The police might see a crime as it was
65 happening or use the video to help in any
consequent investigations.

A security camera (right) allows security personnel to scan faces in a crowd.

Then Tampa **modified** those cameras to
link directly to the police department's own
database. This made them true biometric
70 tools. Instead of humans **analyzing** a video
to see who was depicted, machines did the
identifying.

Computers will do similar analyses of
the crowds at soccer's World Cup tournament
75 in Brazil in 2014. Brazil's system will be even
more advanced, however, with cameras that
are worn like glasses by the police and that
feed into a database of more than 13 million
faces.

80 Advocates of biometric systems say this makes
the system more scientific. Computers can
compare exact measurements of facial features in
order to make matches. Opponents of such
systems object. They argue that machines are
85 easily fooled by such simple **devices** as hats, new
hairstyles, or glasses. Humans are a lot better at
recognizing individuals, they say, than computer
systems are. ∎

Reading Comprehension

Mark each sentence as _T_ (true) or _F_ (false) according to the information in Reading 1. Use the dictionary to help you understand new words.

___ 1. Images of individuals tied to illegal activities were used in looking for criminal activity at the stadium.

___ 2. Security officials felt that using face-recognition technology at the Super Bowl was a good idea.

___ 3. Biometric technology analyzes part of a person's body to determine who he or she is.

___ 4. All the photos in a face-recognition database come from the federal government.

___ 5. Most banks don't use cameras because their customers have complained.

___ 6. Linking the Ybor City system to a police database made the system truly biometric.

___ 7. A face-recognition system helps catch dangerous people who are still unknown to the police.

___ 8. Face-matching systems have no trouble identifying someone wearing a hat or glasses.

READING SKILL   Scanning

LEARN

Most readers remember only general information after reading a text. To find specific information, they go back and _scan_ the reading. _Scanning_ means quickly moving your eyes over the text to find specific things.

One method is to scan for _signals_:

- capital letters: for names of people, cities, countries, and special events
- numbers: for dates, measurements, statistics, and addresses
- symbols: for percentages, monetary amounts, email addresses, etc.
- **bold** or _italic_ type: for words that receive special treatment or emphasis

Another method is to scan for _keywords_:

- specific words related to the information you want to find
- unusual letter groups that your eyes would more easily notice

APPLY

Scan Reading 1 for specific information to answer these questions. Write the answer, the signal(s) or keyword(s) you scanned for, and the line numbers where you found each answer. Compare answers with a partner.

1. At which stadium was the Super Bowl played?

   Answer: *Raymond James Stadium*

   Character(s) or Keyword(s): *capital letters, stadium, Super Bowl*

   Lines: *11*

2. Where is Ybor City?

   Answer: _____

   Character(s) or Keyword(s): _____

   Lines: _____

3. When was the Super Bowl in Tampa, Florida?

   Answer: _____

   Character(s) or Keyword(s): _____

   Lines: _____

4. What is Maine Road Ground?

   Answer: _____

   Character(s) or Keyword(s): _____

   Lines: _____

5. What is a biometric system?

   Answer: _____

   Character(s) or Keyword(s): _____

   Lines: _____

REVIEW A SKILL Finding the Main Idea (See p. 20)

There are nine paragraphs in Reading 1. Which paragraph has each of the following main ideas? Write the number of the paragraph.

___ When cameras were first put up in Ybor City, they helped the police see if crimes were happening.

___ Some people think face-recognition systems take away the privacy of innocent people.

___ Cameras are used at sports stadiums to scan for people who have committed crimes before.

Vocabulary Activities STEP I: Word Level

A. Read these excerpts from an article in a student newspaper on face-recognition technology. For each excerpt, cross out the one word or phrase in parentheses with a different meaning from the other three choices. Compare answers with a partner.

1. Some schools use a card-access security system. In this kind of system, a student must insert a personal ID card into (*a device / a piece of equipment / a piece of data / a machine*) in order to enter the school.

2. The problem is that people lose or forget their cards. A person (*involving / watching / monitoring / guarding*) the entrance will probably not recognize each student, especially at a big school.

3. (*Foreseeing / Anticipating / Predicting / Undertaking*) problems of this type, many schools have turned to "video badging"—using a computer-stored picture of the student as his or her ID card.

4. If a student forgets his or her ID card, the video badge is used as a back-up. A guard or monitor at a computer station (*inside / adjacent to / next to / near*) the entrance can type in the name of a student without a card and see the picture of that student.

5. Many corporate computer networks require employees to type in a password to identify themselves, but there are problems with this system, too. There are lots of ways to steal someone's password. (*Consequently / Therefore / As a result / Justifiably*), restricted information can be accessed by the wrong person.

6. But there's no practical way to steal someone's face. Facial recognition technology (*modifies / analyzes / examines / inspects*) facial features much like a handwriting expert looks at someone's signature.

The word *modify* is similar in meaning to the word *change*. It means "to change something slightly," usually in order to improve it.

The word *device* refers to a tool, machine, or system made for a specific purpose. For example, a knife is a device for cutting things.

CORPUS

B. Check (✓) the items that would be helpful devices for a police officer. In a small group, discuss why you made your choices. Then discuss how each device could be modified for use by people in their homes.

___ 1. a security camera   ___ 5. a high-power flashlight

___ 2. fingerprint powder   ___ 6. a lie detector

___ 3. a police radio   ___ 7. a bicycle

___ 4. portable fences to keep people out of a place   ___ 8. an electronic navigation system, like a GPS

Word Form Chart			
Noun	**Verb**	**Adjective**	**Adverb**
involvement	involve	involved	_____

The word *involve* has the core meaning of "include." The passive verb form usually takes the preposition *in* or *with* and means "to be included or connected." The noun form is *involvement*.

> Mark **was involved in** security efforts at the game.
>
> Her work **involved** testing security systems.
>
> The **involvement** of local police helped reduce crime in the neighborhood.

As an adjective, *involved* has the same meaning as "complicated." It is often used with the word *long* to describe a series of tasks or an event with many parts to it, such as "a long, involved process" or "a long and involved ceremony."

CORPUS

C. Answer the questions using the form of *involve* in parentheses. Refer to Reading 1 for information. Compare answers with a partner.

1. How did they use face-recognition technology at Raymond James Stadium? (*involved*)

   _____

2. Why might a person's photo be in the database of a face-recognition system? (*involvement*)

   _____

3. What places typically use security cameras? (*involved*)

   _____

4. Why is face-recognition technology called "biometric"? (*involve*)

   _____

5. Who might be caught by police using the security system in Ybor City? (*involved in*)

   _____

Word Form Chart			
Noun	**Verb**	**Adjective**	**Adverb**
anticipation	anticipate	anticipatory	_____
consequence consequences	_____	consequent	consequently
controversy	_____	controversial	controversially
justification	justify	justifiable justified justifying unjustified	justifiably
modification	modify	modified modifying unmodified	_____

D. Read these excerpts from another article about face-recognition technology. Then restate each excerpt in your notebook, using the words in parentheses. Do not change the meanings of the sentences. Be prepared to read aloud or discuss your sentences in class.

1. Critics of face-recognition (FR) technology have good reasons to question its accuracy. (*justifiably*)

   *Critics of FR technology **justifiably** question how accurate it can be.*

2. According to one study, the very best FR systems are only about one-third as accurate as human beings. Such findings have fueled a debate within the security industry: Are FR systems a waste of money? (*consequence* or *consequently, controversy*)

3. Developers of FR software cannot know in advance how a face might change from one photo to the next. (*anticipate*)

4. The software is constantly being improved, but image changes caused by aging, lighting, or camera angle still confuse it. (*modify* or *modification*)

5. A human's brain, however, has been practicing recognizing faces since birth. As a result, most people can see past even large changes in another's appearance. (*consequence*)

6. Does it make sense to spend billions of dollars to create automatic FR systems when top-quality "systems" are all around us? (*justified* or *justifiable*)

7. When technicians look ahead to all the possible problems in a human-centered system, most say that it does make sense to create FR systems. (*anticipate* or *anticipation*)

8. A person may be very reliable when full of energy and fully focused on an FR task. But humans do not stay that way for very long. They get tired, stressed out, bored, hungry, sick, distracted, and even angry. All these conditions can greatly affect their reliability. (*consequences*)

9. Although automatic FR systems will always have their opponents, it makes sense to keep improving them and using them. They are a better option than a room full of tired people. (*controversial, modifications*)

Before You Read

Read these questions. Discuss your answers in a small group.

1. Have you ever needed to prove your identity? If so, when? How did you prove it?

2. You probably have at least one picture ID (an identification document with your photograph). It may be a passport, a school ID card, or a driver's license. Do you think the picture looks like you? Why or why not? Do you think the picture could look like someone else?

3. Why might someone try to hide his or her true identity? What techniques would such a person use? Is it always wrong to pretend that you are someone else? Why or why not?

Read

This online news article describes some situations in which people pretend to be someone else.

ID FRAUD

All the places for new students had been taken at a prestigious elementary school in London, England. The school had a waiting list. Any places that opened up would be offered to
5 children at the top of the list. One child (let's call her Wendy) was near, but not at, the top. **Adjacent** to her on the list, one step higher, was another girl (let's call her Jane). Wendy's mother set up an email account in the name
10 of Jane's mother and sent the school an email asking them to remove Jane from the waiting list. **Consequently**, Wendy rose one step. The fraud[1] was discovered when Jane's real mother called the school to ask about the list.
15 By the way, Wendy and Jane were only four years old.

Wendy's mother participated in a small-scale act of Internet fraud. This case of false identity was not very serious—except perhaps to Jane's
20 mother. The school had no effective way of checking identification, probably because it did

Proper identification, such as a passport, can help to prevent identity fraud.

not **anticipate** cheating by desperate parents. It was especially vulnerable to fraud on the Internet, since no face-to-face contact
25 occurred. If Wendy's mother had actually had to go to the school to remove Jane, someone might have recognized her. Even better, if she had been required to show an identification (ID) card, the fraud could probably not have been
30 committed at all.

---

[1] *fraud:* an action in which someone deliberately uses false information to achieve a desirable outcome

FAKE IDS

Her scheme almost worked because she successfully established a false identity, even if only for a short time. Anonymity[2] is a fraudster's best friend, but a fake[3] identity can be the
35 next-best. Establishing someone's true identity is extremely difficult, even beyond the Internet. In most countries, the basic mechanism is a national identification card with a picture and basic personal **data** (address, height, etc.). In
40 some countries (e.g., India, the United States, and the United Kingdom), no national ID card is issued, but driver's licenses typically serve the same purposes. Without a believable ID, you can't get a job, pass through airport security, or even
45 stay at a hotel.

The problem is that fake ID cards are relatively easy to make. In earlier times, cutting out pictures and pasting them on hand-typed cardboard usually did the job. In the 1960s, a
50 teenager named Frank Abagnale, **equipped** only with scissors and a typewriter, made a fake ID that convinced people he was an airline pilot. Now things are not so simple. Modern IDs are almost all made of plastic with numbers and letters
55 pressed onto them by powerful machines, with holograms[4] showing pictures or information, and with magnetic strips on the back. The process to fake an ID card **involves** expensive **equipment** such as presses to stamp the cards, good laser
60 printers to apply type to the plastic, and encoders (**devices** that put information on magnetic strips). Anyone who **undertakes** such expenses probably won't just make one ID for himself or herself. Rather, fakers will sell their services and produce
65 false IDs for other people. They can make a good profit doing this, usually about $92 for every $100 of fake ID sold.

WHO NEEDS FAKES?

In 2004, agents from the U.S. **Federal** Bureau of Investigation (FBI) raided a beauty parlor in
70 Milwaukee, Wisconsin, that was selling a lot more than haircuts. FBI agents said that, while **monitoring** the shop for six months, they had seen beauty shop customers buy passports, birth certificates, driver's licenses, and other identity

75 documents. The FBI did not claim the shop owners actually made the documents but that they earned money by passing them on to customers. Their profit on a valid U.S. passport, for example, was reportedly about $1000.

80 Who would want a false ID? The list is long. An otherwise ordinary person might try to disappear to escape money troubles, a police investigation, an unhappy family life, or some other circumstance by simply moving far away
85 and pretending to be someone else. Some people even stage their own "deaths" so their families can collect money from life insurance policies. First they disappear in some way that **justifies** the assumption that they're dead,
90 such as swimming out to sea and never returning. Then comes the hard part. In order to get a job or rent an apartment somewhere new, they need fake documents. That's where places like the Milwaukee beauty shop come in.

On the Albanian ID card, the fingerprints of the legal holder are encoded on a microchip within the card.

NOT FOR AMATEURS

95 Getting a fake ID is **illegal** and dangerous, perhaps putting a buyer in contact with criminals or leading into a police trap to capture fraudsters. Also, the process often

---

[2] *anonymity:* a situation in which your identity is unknown
[3] *fake:* false
[4] *holograms:* images, created by a laser, that appear to be three-dimensional

goes wrong when an inexperienced person tries

100 it. A man from Hong Kong named Steven Chin Leung had quite a lot of trouble trying to use fake IDs. First, he was charged in the U.S. state of Hawaii for trying to get a U.S. passport **illegally.** To escape those charges, he went to New York

105 and disappeared after the September 11 terrorist attack, when it was impossible to tell who was killed. He was finally caught while trying to get another document—his own death certificate—by **illegally** pretending to be his brother. Authorities

110 knew something was wrong when their research showed that Leung actually had no brothers.

Governments and other issuers of IDs constantly **modify** their systems to stay ahead of the fakers, but it's hard to do. The ID-making **equipment** can

115 be **legally** purchased because it has other, perfectly **legal** uses. Software for putting holograms on ID cards or encoding magnetic strips is easily available on the Internet. Perhaps the future of government IDs can be

120 seen in the new cards issued by the European nation of Albania. In addition to the usual features—picture, signature, and so on—the Albanian card has a biometric[5] ID feature. The fingerprints of the **legal** holder are encoded

125 on a microchip within the card so they can be **analyzed** if there is any **controversy** over whether the ID is valid. The question now is whether the ID fraud industry can find a way to beat even this identification feature.

---

[5] *biometric:* **involving** a measurable characteristic of a person's body

Reading Comprehension

Mark each sentence as *T* (true) or *F* (false) according to the information in Reading 2. Use the dictionary to help you understand new words.

____ 1. Jane's mother pretended to be someone else.

____ 2. The school in London was not very careful in determining parents' identities.

____ 3. In the United States and the United Kingdom., driver's licenses are used as ID cards.

____ 4. In Frank Abagnale's day, it was not technologically possible to make fake IDs.

____ 5. The FBI claimed that people could get fake IDs from a beauty shop in Wisconsin.

____ 6. People who choose to disappear need ID documents to set up new lives as someone else.

____ 7. Life insurance companies help people stage their own "deaths."

____ 8. Steven Chin Leung disappeared in order for his family to collect money from his insurance company.

____ 9. Equipment needed to make fake IDs can be legally purchased in the United States.

____10. Albanian ID cards show the holders' fingerprints but not their picture.

APPLY

Complete the chart by scanning Reading 2 for the answer to each question. Fill in the missing information.

Question	Answer	Signals and Keywords	Lines
1. What is the full name of the FBI?	The Federal Bureau of Investigation	capital letters	68–69
2. What did Wendy's mother send the school?			
3. What word does the abbreviation "ID" stand for?			
4. When did Frank Abagnale make a fake pilot's ID?			
5. If a maker sells an ID for $100, how much profit will he/she make?			
6. What did Steven Chin Leung do in Hawaii?			
7. What country has IDs with biometrics?			

A. Complete the sentences about writer Philip K. Dick by using words from the target vocabulary list. Use each item one time. Use the synonyms in parentheses to help you. (Note: The sentences are not yet in the correct order.)

adjacent	anticipate	involved in	monitor
analyzes	devices	involving	undertook

___ a. The science-fiction author Philip K. Dick, or PKD, had an amazing ability to _____ the effects of future technology on society.
(see in advance)

___ b. Berkeley in the 1950s and 1960s was a center for radical thought and unusual lifestyles. PKD was _____ the area's "beat" poet
(part of)
culture.

___ c. Technological _____ such as face-recognition systems and eye
(tools)
scanners play a special role in PKD's stories.

___ d. He was born in Chicago, Illinois, but he lived most of his life in California. He went to high school in Berkeley, a city _____ to San
(next to)
Francisco.

___ e. In 1974, he began to have disturbing visions, some _____
(including)
dreams of himself as a first-century Roman citizen who was trying to hide from government authorities.

___ f. In 1982, the now-classic movie *Blade Runner* was released. It was based on his story *Do Androids Dream of Electric Sheep?* Like all of Dick's best work, it _____ human identity in a world of powerful machines.
(examines)

___ g. PKD started college in Berkeley, but he dropped out. He worked at a record store until he sold his first short story in 1952. At that point, he _____ fiction writing as a full-time job.
(tried to succeed at)

___ h. These visions shaped his thinking and writing. In some of his books, the main character struggles to break free from technology that helps the government _____ all human action and thought.
(watch over)

B. Tell the story of Philip K. Dick's life by putting the sentences in activity A into a logical order. Number them from *1* to *8* (more than one sequence may be possible). Then use the target words as you compare stories with a partner.

C. Read these sample sentences that feature forms of *analyze*. Then answer the questions that follow, using a dictionary as suggested. Compare answers with a partner.

> a. After we collected information, we had to **analyze** it.
> b. According to government **analysts,** the traffic problem can be solved only by building a new road.
> c. An **analysis** of the neighborhood's water showed several harmful chemicals.
> d. After **analyzing** its purchasing system, the company decided to make some changes.

1. Check (✓) the word closest in meaning to *analyze*. Consult your dictionary before you answer.

   ___ judge

   ___ combine

   ___ examine

   ___ understand

2. Each of the sentences in the box above indicates that something was analyzed. What was analyzed?

   a. _____

   b. _____

   c. _____

   d. _____

3. Look at the sample sentences in your dictionary for *analyze* and its forms. What is being analyzed in each of those samples?

4. Does *analyze* have any forms that are not used in the sample sentences in the box above? If so, what are they? Consult your dictionary.

Vocabulary Activities STEP II: Sentence Level

D. In a small group, discuss these questions. Use a dictionary to clarify word meanings if necessary.

1. Certain criminals try to steal the identities of ordinary people. Which activity might put you in the most danger of having your identity stolen? Why?

   a. shopping online

   b. using a credit card in a hotel

   c. buying something by telephone

   d. answering a survey that asks for your email address

2. Think about a culture you know well. Which of these activities do law enforcement officers monitor? Why?

   a. public gatherings on a holiday

   b. teachers talking to their students

   c. sporting events

   d. buying and selling at shops

3. What might be some consequences of each of these situations? Which consequences are good and which are bad?

   a. losing your ID card

   b. using a security system before it is tested

   c. putting security cameras in a store

   d. using a database of old photos in an FR system

Privacy allows you to live your life without unwanted attention from others. Your privacy is violated when someone—a neighbor, a salesperson, an email spammer, or the government—learns too much about you or what you are doing. Opponents of automated FR and other security technology say it threatens personal privacy. Supporters of the technology say that some violations of privacy are necessary to make society safe. The controversy is about priorities: Is public security more important than personal privacy?

CORPUS

E. In each of these situations, there has been some loss of personal privacy. Write *Y* in the blank when you think the loss of privacy is justified. Write *N* when you think the loss of privacy is not justified. In your notebook, write a short explanation for each of your answers. Be prepared to read aloud or discuss your opinions in class.

___ 1. The police set up cameras to watch people throughout the city.

___ 2. Security cameras at a sporting event take pictures of everyone who enters the stadium.

___ 3. A school takes a picture of each of its students.

___ 4. A school sells pictures of its students to an advertising agency looking for models.

___ 5. Pictures of criminals are loaded into a database.

___ 6. Pictures of everyone who has a driver's license are loaded into a database.

___ 7. A country requires everyone who lives there to get a national ID.

___ 8. A hotel requires you to show an ID card before it will give you a room.

F. Look at these arguments for and against the use of face-recognition technology in public places. Restate each idea in your notebook, using the word in parentheses. Then write a paragraph that expresses your own opinion. Try to use as many target words as possible in your work. Be prepared to present your work or debate the issue in class.

For	Against
The security of the public is more important than the privacy of the individual. Some loss of privacy is necessary to keep people safe. (*justified*)	The government should protect all individual rights, including the right to privacy. Citizens should not have to give up their rights in order to be safe. (*justified*)
Small weaknesses in security can lead to horrible things. Think of September 11. A little more watchfulness could have saved thousands of lives. (*consequences*)	The horrible events of September 11 should not distract us from our ideals. The worst possible effect of such terrorism would be the loss of our basic freedoms. (*consequences*)
Technology can be powerful enough to catch the bad guys without affecting innocent people. We should keep improving face-recognition systems to fulfill their potential. (*undertake* and *devices*)	Face-recognition systems will always make a lot of mistakes. It would be a waste of time to try making a system sensitive enough to all the changes that can occur in a person's appearance. (*undertake* and *devices*)

G. Self-Assessment Review: Go back to page 33 and reassess your knowledge of the target vocabulary. How has your understanding of the words changed? What words do you feel most comfortable with now?

Writing and Discussion Topics

Write about or discuss the following topics.

1. Privacy experts are worried that face-recognition technology will enable the government to monitor the lives of people unnecessarily. Do you share this concern or not? Explain your answer by referring to specific aspects of the average person's life (sleeping, meeting with friends, emailing, etc.).

2. Imagine a face-recognition database that includes a picture of everyone with a driver's license or a passport. Consider the advantages and disadvantages. Whose pictures would you include in a "perfect" database?

3. Some people claim that the best biometric system is genetic. They point out that police and the courts use DNA to make extremely accurate identifications. ID cards with a person's genetic information may someday be created. Do you think such a system would be good or bad? What benefits do you anticipate? What problems?

UNIT 4

How Could They Do That?

In this unit, you will

> read about two remarkable figures in English literature, William Shakespeare and Joseph Conrad.
> review scanning.
> increase your understanding of the target academic words for this unit.

READING SKILL Outlining

Self-Assessment

Think about how well you know each target word, and check (✓) the appropriate column. I have...

TARGET WORDS	never seen the word before	seen the word but am not sure what it means	seen the word and understand what it means	used the word, but am not sure if correctly	used the word confidently in *either* speaking *or* writing	used the word confidently in *both* speaking *and* writing
AWL						
accumulate						
🔑 adequate						
🔑 author						
🔑 debate						
🔑 depress						
🔑 indicate						
🔑 invest						
persist						
precede						
protocol						
reluctance						
sustain						
🔑 text						
🔑 volume						

🔑 Oxford 3000™ keywords

Before You Read

Read these questions. Discuss your answers in a small group.

1. Have you ever seen or read a famous play? Briefly describe it.

2. Who was William Shakespeare? Why is he famous?

3. How would you feel if you found out that a book by your favorite writer was actually written by someone else? Would it matter to you? Why or why not?

MORE WORDS YOU'LL NEED

hoax: a trick that is played on somebody
multilingual: able to use more than one language
noble: belonging to a high social class in a country with a king or queen

Read

Read this section from a chapter in a book about literary history. It describes two points of view about the authorship of William Shakespeare's plays.

Could Shakespeare Have Written Shakespeare's Plays?

Literary detectives have uncovered many facts about William Shakespeare. Still, the most important question of all remains: Did he really write the Shakespeare plays?
5 Sir Francis Bacon, Christopher Marlowe, the Earl of Southampton (Shakespeare's patron), and even Queen Elizabeth herself have at times been suspected of writing them. The sheer **volume** of Shakespeare's work—37 plays,
10 154 sonnets, 2 other poems, and an elegy—has led to suggestions that "William Shakespeare" was actually several people, not one.

OXFORD VS. STRATFORD

The strongest current **debate** is between groups known as the Oxfordians and the
15 Stratfordians. Oxfordians say that Edward de Vere, the 17th Earl of Oxford, wrote the plays under the pen name[1] William Shakespeare. Stratfordians, on the other hand, say that the works were all written by William Shakespeare,
20 an actor known to have been born at Stratford

in 1564. The challenge for both sides is to produce solid evidence. So far, neither side has come up with much.

THE OXFORDIANS' CASE

Oxfordians say the actor Shakespeare was too
25 poorly educated to have been the **author** of the plays. He was the son of a tradesman, and there is no record that he had any schooling. There is no evidence that he ever traveled outside southern England. He was just an actor and an
30 occasional real-estate **investor**. His will[2] mentions no writings, and there is no evidence he ever owned a book. A background like that could not have been **adequate** for writing such brilliant plays. The life of Edward de Vere, on
35 the other hand, was more than **adequate.** His education was the best money could buy. He was very familiar with England's noble families. He traveled to many of the locations important in Shakespeare's plays, including France,
40 Scotland, and Italy.

---

[1] *pen name:* a name, other than his or her legal one, that a writer chooses to use when publishing works
[2] *will:* a document that distributes someone's possessions after he or she dies

William Shakespeare   **Edward de Vere**

The de Vere theory gained a lot of support after 1991. In that year, researchers began studying the handwritten notes in de Vere's copy of a 1569 edition of the Bible. About 1,000 Bible
45 passages are underlined or otherwise marked. Nearly 25 percent of them match up with parts of Shakespeare's work. Probably not a coincidence, say the Oxfordians. For example, part of Act V in *The Merchant of Venice* speaks
50 of a good deed shining out "in a naughty[3] world." One of the passages de Vere underlined in his Bible contains the phrase, "a naughty and crooked nation, among whom ye shine as lights in the world."

THE STRATFORDIANS' CASE

55 Stratfordians reply, "Why look beyond William Shakespeare of Stratford?" He was not the backward son of a lowly family, as many claim. His father was a prosperous merchant who held the town's highest office (high
60 bailiff). The King's New School in Stratford offered an excellent education. Although school records cannot be found, it is likely that the town's high bailiff sent his son there. Shakespeare moved to London in the late
65 1580s, in his early twenties. There he became famous and wealthy as an actor and as London's leading playwright. And certain aspects of his life seem to match better with the plays than de Vere's do. For example, the
70 perceptive portrayal of emotional **depression** in *Hamlet* seems to **indicate** that the **author** had experienced the ailment. *Hamlet* was written around the year 1600, four years after William Shakespeare's only son, Hamnet, died
75 at the age of 11.

Stratfordians also point out that the de Vere theory assumes an unlikely hoax. The Oxford camp claims that de Vere wanted to hide his **authorship** because it went against **protocol** for
80 the noble class. A highborn earl simply should not be writing plays for common people. To give de Vere cover, William Shakespeare of Stratford must have agreed (probably for pay) to serve as a front man[4]. The Stratfordians point out that,
85 for this to be true, Shakespeare's many friends and acquaintances were either blind enough to be fooled by it or willing to be in on the trick. The same goes for de Vere's friends and acquaintances, including the very intelligent
90 Queen Elizabeth. The part hardest to believe is that a plan like that could be **sustained** for decades without the secret being revealed.

Another difficulty for the Oxfordians is that the 17th Earl of Oxford died in 1604. Many of
95 the greatest plays were produced after this date. *Macbeth*, for example, dates from 1606–1607 and *The Tempest* from 1611. A great deal of careful work has confirmed these dates, and most Oxfordians **reluctantly** concede that de Vere's
100 death **preceded** the appearance of these plays. But the Oxford camp **persists** in their position. They argue that de Vere wrote them before he died and that they were brought out as needed for performance. In addition, the **texts** of many
105 Shakespeare plays contain references to events after 1604. The Oxfordians say someone must have added contemporary references to make the plays look timely.

Queen Elizabeth and Edward de Vere as portrayed in the 2011 movie *Anonymous*

---

[3] *naughty:* bad; disobedient; rude
[4] *front man:* a person who agrees to pretend to be someone else in the eyes of the public

Any **debate** centered on speculation alone will probably last a very long time. Neither side in this **debate** seems likely to **accumulate** the evidence necessary to settle the matter. As one researcher, Al Austin, summarizes the controversy, "Those who believe de Vere was Shakespeare must accept an improbable hoax as part of it, a conspiracy of silence involving, among others, Queen Elizabeth herself. Those who side with the Stratford man must believe in miracles." ■

Reading Comprehension

Mark each sentence as *T* (true) or *F* (false) according to the information in Reading 1. Use the dictionary to help you understand new words.

___ 1. There is serious debate about whether Shakespeare's plays were really written by Edward de Vere.

___ 2. Unlike Shakespeare, de Vere is known to have traveled to locations important in the plays.

___ 3. Stratfordians say that even though Shakespeare was uneducated, he taught himself enough to have written the plays.

___ 4. About one-quarter of the Bible passages that de Vere highlighted are very similar to passages in Shakespearean plays.

___ 5. Oxfordians say that Shakespeare agreed to pretend that he wrote the plays, even though de Vere really wrote them.

___ 6. Many Shakespearean plays first appeared after de Vere's death.

___ 7. Stratfordians say it's unlikely de Vere could have hidden his authorship from so many people for so long.

___ 8. New evidence is likely to settle the Oxford–Stratford debate within the next few years.

READING SKILL   Outlining

LEARN

One way to better understand a reading is to outline it. Outlining helps you see how the text is organized so that you can figure out the main ideas and details.

In a common outlining system, Roman numerals (I, II, III, etc.) show the major ideas or sections in a reading. The next level of detail is indicated with capital letters.

The outlining system becomes more involved as the complexity of a text increases. For more information on outlining, go online and do a search for "how to outline."

APPLY

Complete the outline of Reading 1 with phrases from the box.

Details of the Oxfordian position
Evidence from the 1556 Bible
Shakespeare's likely attendance at a good school
Matching Shakespeare's plays with his life

The problem of de Vere's 1604 death
Shakespeare's weak background
Stratfordian position

Could Shakespeare Have Written Shakespeare's Plays?

I.   Introduction

II. General description of the Oxford–Stratford debate

    A. Oxfordian position

    B. _____

III. *Details of the Oxfordian position* _____

    A. _____

    B. de Vere's strong background

    C. _____

IV. Details of the Stratfordian position

    A. Prominence of Shakespeare's family

    B. _____

    C. Shakespeare's prosperity and importance in London

    D. _____

    E. An unlikely hoax necessary for Oxfordian position

V.   _____

    A. Dates of plays after 1604

    B. Oxfordian explanations

VI. Likely future of the debate

REVIEW A SKILL Scanning (See p. 36)

(See p. 36)

Scan Reading 1 for specific years. Answer the questions.

1. When was Shakespeare born?
2. When did the Earl of Oxford die?
3. When was *The Tempest* first produced?

A. Read these excerpts from another article about Shakespeare's work. For each excerpt, cross out the one word or phrase in parentheses with a different meaning from the other three choices. Compare answers with a partner.

1. None of Shakespeare's plays has survived as a manuscript in the (*author's / sculptor's / writer's / playwright's*) own handwriting. Consequently, we do not know for certain which words Shakespeare actually wrote.

2. Unfortunately, printing companies at the time were not very reliable. Errors usually (*built up / accumulated / occurred / multiplied*) in a work during the stages of preparation for printing.

3. Errors were also introduced by the people who set the type. They might change what a manuscript said just because their supply of letters was not (*relevant / sufficient / enough / adequate*) to spell what the author wrote.

4. We have no way of knowing how to fix the errors. For example, the earliest printed (*texts / copies / protocols / versions*) of *King Lear* and *Richard III* are obviously incorrect, but we have no way of knowing how to restore them to Shakespeare's original versions.

The word *precede* means "come before" or "happen earlier than." The first step in a process precedes the second step. The second step precedes the third. Viewed another way, the second step *follows* the first.

CORPUS

B. Check (✓) the statements that correctly describe the order of events in Reading 1. Rewrite the unchecked sentences and correct the order. Discuss your answers with a partner.

___ 1. The writing of *Hamlet* preceded the writing of *Macbeth*.

___ 2. De Vere's death preceded Shakespeare's.

___ 3. Shakespeare's move to London followed his rise to fame.

___ 4. The publication of de Vere's Bible preceded Shakespeare's birth.

___ 5. The publication of *Hamlet* followed the death of Shakespeare's son.

___ 6. De Vere's death followed the production of *The Tempest*.

The word *protocol* refers to the system of rules for correct behavior. It is often used in formal, official contexts. People can *follow protocol, go against protocol,* or *break protocol.*

*Many say he broke **protocol** when he preceded the president into the room.*

Note: Today, *protocol* also refers to the set of signals and rules that control how information is sent from one computer to another. For example, the abbreviation *http* at the beginning of many website addresses stands for "hypertext transfer protocol."

CORPUS

C. Match each type of protocol with an example. Compare answers with a partner. Then write an example of your own for each type of protocol in your notebook.

___ 1. military protocol

___ 2. social protocol

___ 3. research protocol

___ 4. business protocol

___ 5. medical protocol

___ 6. meeting protocol

a. Type the words in the SEARCH field and put quotation marks around them in order to get the most relevant hits.

b. All managers must explain company email policies to new employees on their first day of work.

c. Never turn your back on an officer without first saluting and having that salute returned.

d. Speaker A has two minutes. Then Speaker B has one minute to address Speaker A's points.

e. To the bride, you say, "Good luck." To the groom, you say, "Congratulations."

f. Take one pill every six hours for four days then reduce the dosage to one pill every twelve hours for two days.

Vocabulary Activities | STEP II: Sentence Level

Word Form Chart			
Noun	**Verb**	**Adjective**	**Adverb**
accumulation	accumulate	accumulated	_____
author	author	authorial	authorially
debate	debate	debatable	debatably
sustenance sustainability	sustain	sustainable sustained	sustainably
volume	_____	voluminous	voluminously

D. Read another article about Shakespeare's works. Then restate the sentences in your notebook, using the words in parentheses. Be prepared to read aloud or discuss your sentences in class.

1. After Shakespeare's death, actors John Heminge and Henry Condell collected copies of his plays. (*author*)

   After Shakespeare's death, Heminge and Condell collected copies of the **author***'s plays.*

2. Within seven years of Shakespeare's death in 1616, they had put together one of the landmark publications in English literature, the *First Folio*. It contained 36 of his plays. (*voluminous*)

3. Several unauthorized versions of each play, called "foul copies," were in circulation. No one could say for sure how these compared to what Shakespeare intended. (*debatable*)

4. Heminge and Condell knew Shakespeare extremely well, having worked with him over the course of many years. They were in a good position to separate good versions from bad ones. (*sustained*)

5. Still, they had not worked on every play with Shakespeare. Some foul copies were probably close to accurate, but how could they tell? Errors tended to give birth to other errors. (*accumulated*)

6. Heminge and Condell did their best, and 1623 marked the release of 700 copies of the 900-page *Mr. William Shakespeares Comedies, Histories & Tragedies. Published according to the True Originall Copies.* (*volume*)

E. Read the story in activity D again. Imagine you are a journalist who, after all these years, is able to interview William Shakespeare about the *First Folio* and other editions of his plays. Prepare interview questions, using the cues provided, and write them in your notebook. Be prepared to act out your interview with a partner.

1. what / text

   What is your opinion of the texts included in the First Folio?

2. how / invest

3. how / sustain

4. what / adequate

5. who / author

Word Form Chart			
Noun	**Verb**	**Adjective**	**Adverb**
indication indicator	indicate	indicative indicated	_____

F. Write the answers to the questions in your notebook, using the form of *indicate* in parentheses. Refer to Reading 1 for information. Compare sentences with a partner.

1. Why do most scholars agree that whoever wrote the Shakespeare plays must have had a good education? (*indicative*)

2. What is the significance of Shakespeare's father having been the high bailiff of Stratford? (*indicate*)

3. Why are the highlighted passages in Edward de Vere's Bible important? (*indication*)

4. What is the relationship between the lack of solid evidence and the probable length of the debate ? (*indicator*)

Before You Read

Read these questions. Discuss your answers in a small group.

1. How many languages can you speak or write? Are you more comfortable speaking them or writing them?

2. What is the best way for you to expand your vocabulary in a second or third language? Reading? Listening? Real-world interactions? Observing others?

Read

This online article examines some possible reasons for Joseph Conrad's exceptional ability to write in English, which he learned only as an adult.

Fame in a Foreign Language: Joseph Conrad

Joseph Conrad

Literary success is hard enough to achieve in one's native language. Very few **authors** can **sustain** themselves on money earned through writing. For a nonnative speaker of a language, literary success in that

15 language is extremely rare. Yet the English-language novels of Joseph Conrad **indicate** that it is not impossible.

Conrad was born Jozef Teodor Konrad Korzeniowski in 1857, in an area of present-day

20 Ukraine that was then a part of Poland. He was born into a noble family that owned a good deal of land. Russia ruled Poland at the time, and both of Conrad's parents took part in the struggle for independence. Conrad's father was

25 arrested in 1861 for revolutionary activity, and the family was exiled to the remote city of

Vologda, in northern Russia. The long winters and difficult living conditions there were too much for Conrad's mother. She died of

30 tuberculosis when Conrad was only seven years old. His father's health suffered, too. The Russian government finally allowed the father and son to return to Poland, to the city of Krakow, but the father soon died. Conrad

35 was eleven at the time.

EARLY LANGUAGE EXPERIENCE

His early life with his parents almost certainly influenced his success with languages. His father was clearly good at them—skillful enough to translate written **texts** into Polish

40 from French and English. Like many well-born Poles at the time, Conrad learned French early in life. Given Russia's domination of Poland and his family's exile in Russia, Conrad must have learned some Russian as well.

45 He lived with his grandmother after his father's death. He did not **invest** much energy in his schoolwork, including his required classes in Latin and German. Restless and unhappy, he declared at the age of 14 that he

50 wanted to be a sailor. In 1874, at the age of

16, Conrad traveled to France to learn commercial sailing and to avoid being drafted into the Russian army. His French language skills were more than **adequate** for his duties during the four years he
55 spent in the French merchant marine[1]. His career was interrupted by a suicide attempt, perhaps brought on by worry over debts from wild living in the south of France. Conrad recovered, but if he stayed in France the government would probably
60 have turned him over to the Russians for military service. He had to leave, so he went to England.

An English steam ship

He signed on at the age of 20 as a seaman on an English steam ship, but he did not need to speak very much English to get by. Ordinary seamen on
65 vessels like his spoke many different languages and developed their own mixed language to communicate. However, **protocol** in the British merchant marine required ambitious sailors to pass through several levels before commanding a ship.
70 Each level had its own test, in English. By reading in English as much as he could, he became good enough to pass the written tests for second-class seaman, then first-class, then master. He sailed under the flag of Britain for a total of 16 years, and
75 he became a British citizen in 1886.

SPEAKING AND WRITING

Throughout his life, Conrad was more **inclined** to read and write than to speak. He was often **depressed** and socially uncomfortable. This was probably one reason why, despite his excellent
80 skills in English writing, he was very **reluctant** to speak English. A strong Polish accent **persisted** throughout his life. Even his wife and children said it made him hard to understand. French remained

the language he was most comfortable
85 speaking for the rest of his life.

By the time his first novel, *Almayer's Folly*, was published in 1895, there was no doubt that English was the language in which he would write. He had **accumulated** an immense
90 vocabulary. His style was intriguing but not foreign-sounding. In fact, he wrote with a directness and plain style that were about 30 years ahead of their time. Some of his works, especially *Heart of Darkness* (1902) and
95 *Nostromo* (1904), still sound reasonably modern.

Why Conrad became such a master of written English will always be a matter of **debate**. He himself wrote that the rhythms of the language matched some inner sense that had been with
100 him since birth. As he once wrote, "If I had not written in English, I would not have written at all." He never wrote professionally in either of the languages that **preceded** English in his life, Polish and French.

PSYCHOLOGICAL EXPLANATIONS

105 Psychologists have guessed that Conrad associated these other languages with unpleasant experiences—his exile, his parents' deaths, his attempted suicide. Also, the experiences that shaped Conrad's earliest
110 novels were lived in English. English might have been established in Conrad's mind as the language of adult experience. These guesses make a lot of sense. A large **volume** of research **indicates** that multilingual people
115 tend to link some aspects of life with one language and other aspects with another.

By the time he died in 1924, at the age of 67, Conrad had a secure place in 20th-century English literature. He was a personal friend of
120 such greats as H.G. Wells and Ford Madox Ford. Some literary reviewers criticized him for not being "really English," for using French-based vocabulary instead of Anglo-Saxon words (e.g. *arrest* instead of *stop*), or for
125 letting some Polish influences show through his English. Almost no one now remembers who these critics were.

---

[1] *merchant marine:* a group of ships that transport commercial goods but that might, in wartime, support a country's navy

APPLY

Complete this outline of Reading 2 in your own words.

I.   Introduction

II. _____

    A. Birth in Poland
    B. Exile to Russia
    C. Death of parents

III. _____

IV. Conrad's teen years

    A. _____

    B. _____

    C. _____

V.   _____

    A. Lack of need for English as a seaman

    B. _____

    C. Length of service

VI. Conrad's spoken English

VII. _____

VIII. Explanations for Conrad's literary ability in English

    A. _____

    B. _____

IX. Conrad's position in English literature

Reading Comprehension

Mark each sentence as *T* (true) or *F* (false) according to the information in Reading 2.
Use the dictionary to help you understand new words.

___ 1. Joseph Conrad spoke two other languages before he learned English.

___ 2. Conrad didn't invest much energy in school, preferring to go to sea instead.

___ 3. Sailing protocol demanded that any sailor working on a British ship had to pass a large volume of tests in English.

___ 4. Conrad felt that English had a rhythm that matched some inner feeling he had.

___ 5. Most of his novels had to be translated into English from French or Polish.

___ 6. Conrad spoke French, but only reluctantly and not well.

___ 7. Conrad may have written in English because he associated the language with experiences in his adult life.

A. Complete the sentences about synesthesia by using words from the target vocabulary list. Use each item one time. The synonyms in parentheses can help you.

adequate	debate	persisted	reluctant
authors	indicates	precedes	

1. Joseph Conrad and Vladimir Nabokov, two famous _____ , each
   (writers)
   had a form of synesthesia—a condition in which two or more senses, such as
   hearing and sight, work together.

2. The most common form of synesthesia involves a link between music and
   colors. The sound of a musical note _____ the visual perception
   (comes earlier than)
   of color.

3. Conrad said that he preferred to write in English because it matched an inner
   sense of rhythm that had _____ ever since his childhood.
   (continued)

4. Nabokov's autobiography, *Speak, Memory,* _____ that he
   (shows)
   perceived letters as colors. For example, the sound of the letter "i" was white
   and the letter "c" was light blue.

5. Among researchers, there is much _____ about whether the
   (argument)
   brain activity that happens during synesthesia is related to language ability.

6. Most scientists are _____ to claim a clear connection between
   (unwilling)
   synesthesia and language because they lack _____
   (enough)
   experimental evidence.

B. Many academic words are also considered formal words. Which of the target words in this unit (see the chart on page 49) are more formal synonyms for these informal words? Be sure to use the right form of the target words.

Informal	Formal
1. continue	_____
2. deep sadness	_____
3. enough	_____
4. show	_____
5. amount	_____
6. writer	_____

C. Read these sample sentences that feature forms of *precede*. Then answer the questions that follow, using a dictionary as suggested. Compare answers with a partner.

> a. In the life cycle of a butterfly, the larva stage **precedes** the pupa stage.
> b. If we let one person skip the test, it will set a bad **precedent,** and everyone will ask to skip it.
> c. Crops failed that year because, in **preceding** years, very little rain had fallen.
> d. In a well-run university, the best interests of the students take **precedence** over all other concerns.

1. Check (✓) the word closest in meaning to *precede*. Consult a dictionary before you answer.

___ supersede

___ predate

___ validate

___ forestall

2. Look at the sample sentences in your dictionary for *precede* and its forms. In each of those samples, what is coming before something else?

_____

3. Does *precede* have any forms that are not used in the sample sentences in the box above? If so, what are they? Consult your dictionary.

_____

D. Discuss these questions in a small group. Use a dictionary to clarify word meanings if needed.

1. Which of these possible discoveries could resolve the debate about the authorship of Shakespeare's plays? (You may choose more than one.)

   a. copies printed before Shakespeare's death

   b. handwritten copies of the plays

   c. a book by someone in Shakespeare's time crediting him with the plays

   d. Shakespeare's diary

2. Think about your own writing in a language other than your native language. Which of these aspects of writing is the hardest for you? Why?

   a. finding exactly the right word

   b. correctly using the vocabulary you already know

   c. finding a native-like organization

   d. developing a style that keeps your readers interested

3. What might be some consequences of each situation? Which consequences are good and which are bad? Explain your answers.

   a. investing your money in a new business

   b. investing your time as a volunteer

   c. reading a depressing book

   d. going against protocol by wearing shorts to school or work

The verb *depress* means "to cause to sink to a lower position." The adjective is *depressed*, and the noun form is *depression*. These words can be used in many contexts:

Physical   *He **depressed** the DELETE key to erase the document.*

Business   *The warm weather **depressed** the skiing industry for months.*

Economics   *During a **depression,** the unemployment rate increases.*

The most common context is emotional. *Depressed* can mean simply sad or it can refer to a medical condition in which chemicals in the brain are out of balance, causing constant sadness.

Sad   *He's very **depressed** about his grades. He might not finish the class.*

         *That film was **depressing**. Let's do something fun to lighten the mood.*

Clinical   *She has suffered from **depression** since she was a teenager.*

         *It's hard for someone who is clinically **depressed** to hold a job.*

CORPUS

E. On a scale from *1* (most depressing) to *10* (not at all depressing), rate each of these things. Discuss your ratings in a small group.

___ 1. adventure movies

___ 2. a big family gathering

___ 3. the last day of school

___ 4. spending the day alone

___ 5. looking at pictures from your childhood

___ 6. remembering a friend whom you don't see anymore

___ 7. rainy, cold weather

___ 8. moving to a new city

F. Look at these arguments for and against considering a writer's personal life when evaluating his or her work. Restate each idea in your notebook, using some form of the word in parentheses. Then write a paragraph that expresses your own opinion. Use as many target words as possible in your work. Be prepared to read your paragraph or debate this issue in class.

For	Against
A writer's basic view of the world is determined by his or her experiences. Of course this affects the writer's approach. (*indicate*)	The same experience can affect different writers differently. We can only guess at its influence. If our guesses are wrong, we may misunderstand the work. (*reluctant*)
Writers often base the characters in their works on real people. Unless we know who these people are and what relationships they had to the author, we can't fully understand the work. (*text*)	A literary character is never exactly like a real person. Thinking about real people when you read keeps you from seeing the character as the author has developed it. (*persist*)
You can only know whether an author's handling of a topic is reliable by evaluating his or her experience. For example, Herman Melville's writing about whales in *Moby Dick* seems more reliable once you know that Melville used to work on ships. (*adequate*)	Reliability doesn't necessarily depend on experience. A good author can write about something well without ever experiencing it. For example, an author can easily write about emotional problems without having them. (*depression*)

G. Self-Assessment Review: Go back to page 49 and reassess your knowledge of the target vocabulary. How has your understanding of the words changed? What words do you feel most comfortable with now?

Writing and Discussion Topics

Write about or discuss the following topics.

1. Joseph Conrad could work as a seaman on British ships without knowing much English. Describe two or three other foreign-language settings in which someone could work without knowing much of the language.

2. Think of written works in the language you know best. Can you tell when one has been written by a foreigner? If so, how? Describe some specific features that make a piece of writing seem foreign.

3. Is a professionally translated book or play just as good as the work in its original language? What are some advantages and disadvantages of reading a work in translation?

UNIT 5

Weather Warnings

In this unit, you will

> read about the role of weather experts in court and about the relationship between weather and climate.

> review outlining.

> increase your understanding of the target academic words for this unit.

READING SKILL Reading Charts and Graphs

Self-Assessment

Think about how well you know each target word, and check (✓) the appropriate column. I have...

TARGET WORDS	never seen the word before	seen the word but am not sure what it means	seen the word and understand what it means	used the word, but am not sure if correctly	used the word confidently in *either* speaking *or* writing	used the word confidently in *both* speaking *and* writing
AWL						
🔑 assist						
coherent						
🔑 core						
🔑 energy						
🔑 ensure						
🔑 exhibit						
🔑 interval						
orient						
phenomenon						
🔑 previous						
reinforce						
🔑 route						
🔑 section						
🔑 strategy						

🔑 Oxford 3000™ keywords

Outside the Reading What do you know about meteorology? Watch the video on the student website to find out more.

65

Before You Read

Read these questions. Discuss your answers in a small group.

1. What is the weather like at your school or university today? How do you know? What was it like on this date last year? If you don't know, how could you find out?

2. Name some ways in which weather affects business. In what ways is bad weather expensive?

3. How might weather play a role in solving crimes?

MORE WORDS YOU'LL NEED

court: a location in which public arguments about legal issues take place

forecast: a prediction of future events; often used in reference to weather

hail: frozen rain that falls in hard, round balls, even in warm weather

Read

This online news article explains how weather data is helping settle court cases.

The Weather Goes to Court: Forensic Meteorology

The witness testified that she had heard the defendant confess to stealing a car. She was sitting on a park bench, she said, when the defendant, speaking loudly and pointing forcefully
5 toward the parking lot, told another man he had just "jacked[1] that silver Toyota." She said she could easily overhear it because the defendant was standing only about 50 yards northeast of her. She knew it was him because he was on a
10 small hill where she could easily see him. The prosecutor thanked her and she sat down.

It was the defense attorney's turn. His **strategy** was to make the jury doubt what they had just heard. He called a new witness, a meteorologist.
15 People throughout the courtroom wondered: Why call a weather expert?

The expert confidently stated that it had been sunny with excellent visibility on the day in

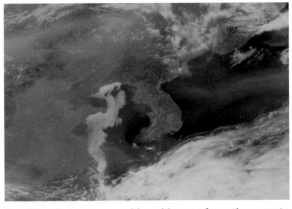

Satellite photos can provide evidence of weather events.

question. Weather records said so. Could the
20 **previous** witness have seen the defendant talking? The weather would not have been a problem, the expert said. Could she have overheard what he said? "Well, the way she described it, probably not. The wind was a bit

---

[1] *jacked:* slang for "stolen"

25 strong that day, out of the southwest at about 15 miles per hour. He was northeast of her and standing on a hill. Sound waves heading into wind get pushed upward. By the time they had traveled 50 yards, they would have been too high to reach
30 her ears."

WEATHER "BACKCASTS"

This case **exhibits** how meteorology can be considered a branch of forensic science. The term *forensics* comes from a Latin word that means "arguing for or against a position." In common
35 modern usage, it means "the practice of discovering material that can be used in court cases or other disputes." Sciences from anthropology to zoology have been put to forensic use. Forensic meteorology can contribute to the
40 picture of the conditions surrounding a crime or an accident. Rather than providing a forecast of what the weather might be in the future, forensic meteorologists specialize in "backcasts" of what the weather was at a given time in the past.

CAREFUL RECORDS

45 Weather **phenomena** have been measured and carefully recorded for hundreds of years. In the United States and many other countries, daily records of air temperature, sky conditions, precipitation[2], and wind are available for almost
50 any inhabited place. What was the weather in New York like for George Washington's 1789 inauguration as the first president? Clear skies with a high temperature of 59° Fahrenheit.

THE VALUE OF AN EXPERT

Anyone with an Internet connection can find that
55 information in five minutes, without any **assistance** from a highly paid meteorologist. An expert's true value is presenting data to **orient** you to the general circumstances and then interpreting that data and pointing out
60 possibilities. The expert analysis draws scattered facts together into a **coherent** picture.

For example, imagine that a farmer wants his insurance company to pay for storm damage to his crops. A large **section** of his cornfield has
65 been flattened. Official records say hail fell that day. He blames the hail for the damage to his crops, and his policy clearly covers hail damage.

His insurance company disputes the **core** argument of his case—that the damage was
70 done by hail. The company denies the claim. The farmer, moved to action by the prospect of collecting tens of thousands of dollars, takes the company to court.

The insurance
75 company calls in a forensic meteorologist. The company's lawyer shows
80 photographs of the farmer's damaged corn-stalks, which all fell to
85 the ground in the same direction. The destructive **energy** of hail,
90 she testifies, produces damage from above, not from the side. She also says that sophisticated radar data show that the storm, as it passed over the farm, lacked the strong updrafts needed
95 to produce hail. Hail was recorded at the weather station 30 miles away, about six minutes before the storm reached the farm. But in that short **interval**, the character of the storm changed. This evidence has given the
100 judge strong doubts about the farmer's claim. These doubts are **reinforced** when the meteorologist explains that radar data also show an extremely strong burst of wind at the farm's location. The judge eventually rules
105 that the crop damage was caused not by hail but by wind. The farmer's policy does not cover wind damage.

Hail from a thunderstorm damages crops.

QUALIFICATIONS

The tools of forensic meteorology continually get more precise, more affordable, and easier
110 to use. Any eager entrepreneur who wants to start a weather-consulting business can buy and operate the necessary equipment. So what **ensures** that someone claiming to be a

---

[2] *precipitation:* moisture from the air that falls to the ground, e.g., rain or snow

forensic meteorologist really is? Neither the federal government nor any state officially licenses meteorologists. The best **route** to professional status is to earn the title of Certified Consulting Meteorologist from the American Meteorological Society (AMS). Experts with that credential have demonstrated to the AMS that they know what they are doing and are honest. Those are very good qualities to have when you step up to the witness stand in a court of law.

Reading Comprehension

Mark each sentence as *T* (true) or *F* (false) according to the information in Reading 1. Use the dictionary to help you understand new words.

___ 1. Sound waves have enough energy to travel straight through a strong wind.

___ 2. Meteorologists often act as judges in court.

___ 3. Forensic scientists discover and interpret evidence to use in court cases.

___ 4. George Washington became president of the United States on a sunny day in New York.

___ 5. Weather records for previous years are available only to certified meteorologists.

___ 6. Hail typically has a downward orientation, not a sideways orientation.

___ 7. Only records at an official weather station can be introduced in court.

___ 8. An insurance policy might cover one type of weather phenomenon but not another.

___ 9. A forensic meteorologist must have a license from the federal or state government.

___10. A professional organization certifies meteorologists to ensure that they have competency in the core areas of meteorological science.

READING SKILL　Reading Charts and Graphs

LEARN

A reading text may include a chart or a graph to show relationships among ideas. A chart usually has vertical columns and horizontal rows. A graph looks more like a picture, such as a set of lines, an arrangement of bars, or a circle divided into sections.

APPLY

Look at the graph showing average temperature and precipitation data for a city in the midwestern United States. Answer the questions that follow in your notebook. Compare answers with a partner.

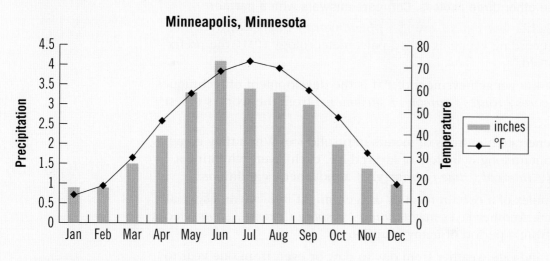

Minneapolis, Minnesota

1. What is the coldest month in Minneapolis ?
2. What is the warmest month?
3. What is the wettest month?
4. What are the driest months?
5. In which months are the average precipitation levels the same?
6. In which two months are the average temperatures the same?
7. What is the relationship between average temperature and precipitation?
8. If you were going to visit Minneapolis, when would you go? Why?

REVIEW A SKILL Outlining (See p. 52)

Review the Reading Skill material about outlines in Unit 4. Add more detail to this outline from "The Weather Goes to Court: Forensic Meteorology."

I.   A sample case

_____

II. What forensic meteorology is

_____

III. Weather records

_____

IV. The value of an expert

_____

V.   Qualifications

_____

A. Read these excerpts from a college textbook about meteorology. For each excerpt, cross out the one word or phrase in parentheses with a different meaning from the other three choices. Compare answers with a partner.

1. The study of weather (*extremes / events / phenomena / happenings*) before humans began recording events is called paleometeorology (PM), the prefix *paleo-* meaning "old."

2. Perhaps the best-known achievement of PM is the development of techniques for reading ice (*cores / routes / samples / specimens*) from the world's oldest ice fields.

3. Tubular drills penetrate hundreds of meters into solid ice. When they come back up, they contain long cylinders of layered ice, each layer exhibiting a distinct (*period / interval / time / strategy*) of atmospheric conditions.

4. In one layer, bubbles of a certain form of oxygen might indicate an especially warm set of years. Another layer may (*exhibit / display / orient / show*) flecks of volcanic ash from a period of many eruptions.

5. Ice cores cannot indicate weather from day to day, or even from one year to the next. Instead, they (*assist / reinforce / aid / help*) scientists in seeing long-term changes over periods of hundreds of years.

6. Ice cores are used with other indicators of climatic conditions to develop a(n) (*unified / coherent / engaging / integrated*) account of what happened on the Earth before weather data was recorded.

7. For example, many scientists claim that from about 800 CE to 1100 CE, the climate was unusually warm. Evidence of plant life, core samples of soil, erosion patterns in rocks, and accounts of human activity all (*indicate / reinforce / confirm / strengthen*) this claim.

8. The end of the warm weather (*ensured / energized / guaranteed / made it certain*) that plants and animals could no longer live as far north as they had in previous centuries.

B. What did you do (or what do you usually do) in the interval between these events? List as many things as you can in your notebook. Discuss your list with a partner. How similar are your results?

1. the interval between very cold weather and very warm weather

2. the interval between finishing one school year and starting another

3. the interval between the first and second acts of a play

4. the interval between taking a test and getting the results

5. the interval between something bad you did as a child and your parent(s) finding out about it

6. the interval between sending an important text message and waiting for the reply

The word *strategy* means "plan of action." It is used mostly in the context of government or business, but individuals can also have personal strategies for accomplishing things.

C. Imagine you want to find out what the weather was like on the day and in the place your mother was born. Check (✓) the strategies you would use. For each strategy you check, be prepared to say how it might be useful and what difficulties it might present. Discuss your answers with a partner.

___ 1. examine the rings of a tree trunk

___ 2. talk to very old people

___ 3. visit the headquarters of the National Weather Service

___ 4. do an Internet search

___ 5. visit the library at your school or university

___ 6. talk to your mother or father

Vocabulary Activities | STEP II: Sentence Level

Word Form Chart			
Noun	**Verb**	**Adjective**	**Adverb**
energy	energize	energetic	energetically

In this unit, *energy* refers to forces or sources of power in the environment. Heat, coal, gas, wind, and water can all be sources of energy.

> The **energy** from the storm originated in the Pacific Ocean.

When *energy* is used to refer to people, it means "the ability to be very active" or "to activate something or someone."

> People usually have less **energy** in hot weather.

> The cool weather has really **energized** me to finish the work in the garden.

D. Write answers to the questions in your notebook, using the word in parentheses. Refer to Reading 1 for information. Compare answers with a partner.

1. In the opening scenario of Reading 1, what did the witness say she saw? (*energetically*)

   *The witness said she saw the man **energetically** talk about how he had just stolen a car.*

2. According to the meteorologist, why did the witness probably not hear the defendant? (*energy*)

3. Why did the farmer decide to take the insurance company to court? (*energize*)

4. Why does hail do damage to the hood of a car but not the tires? (*energy*)

5. Who can become a forensic meteorologist? (*energetic*)

6. What should a meteorologist understand in order to be certified? (*energy*)

Word Form Chart			
Noun	**Verb**	**Adjective**	**Adverb**
assistance assistant	assist	assisted	_____
coherence	cohere	coherent	coherently
exhibit exhibition	exhibit	_____	_____
phenomenon (plural: phenomena)	_____	phenomenal	phenomenally
section	section	sectional	sectionally

E. Read these sentences about some research on lightning. Then answer the questions that appear after each piece of information in your notebook. In each answer, use a form of the word in parentheses. Be prepared to read aloud or discuss your answers in class.

1. Researchers at Duke University have begun analyzing data for a hypothesis about the connection between lightning and the emission of high-energy gamma rays coming from Earth's own atmosphere.

   What will be the result of all the separate pieces of data? (*coherence*)

   *A **coherent** explanation*

2. Natural emissions of gamma rays—extremely energetic forms of electromagnetic radiation—are usually caused only by high-energy events in space.

   What usually causes emissions of gamma rays? (*phenomenon*)

3. In 1994, scientists detected gamma rays that showed signs of originating near the Earth's surface. And researchers quickly found evidence that those emissions were connected to lightning.

   What was special about the gamma rays found in 1994? (*exhibit*)

4. With the help of the National Science Foundation, the Duke researchers tried to define that connection. They found that, on average, one of these TGFs (terrestrial gamma-ray flashes) occurs about 1.4 seconds before an actual lightning flash.

   How did the Duke researchers get the money and resources to pursue their research? (*assist*)

5. The exact cause of these TGFs remains unclear. The researchers have begun looking at different areas of thunderclouds. They believe something happens near a cloud top during a thunderstorm to create extremely powerful electron beams.

   How are the scientists examining thunderclouds? (*section*)

6. Whatever causes TGFs probably depends on atmospheric occurrences found only in the tropics.

   Why wouldn't scientists be able to find TGFs in Canada? (*phenomenon*)

Before You Read

Read these questions. Discuss your answers in a small group.

1. Think about the weather when you were a child. Does the weather in your hometown now seem different from then? If so, how?

2. In the place you now live, what are the seasons of the year? What are the characteristics of each season?

3. Look at the map and locate these places: Greenland; Iceland; Norway; Canada; Germany; Ukraine; Russia; Cyprus. Write each name in the proper blank. What do you know about these areas?

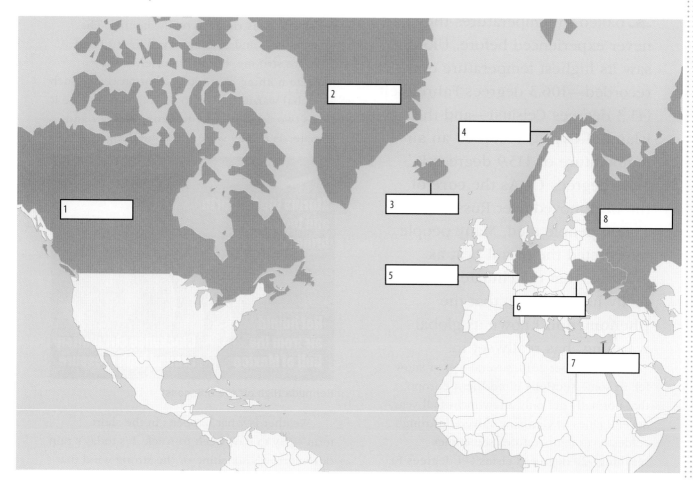

1. _____

2. _____

3. _____

4. _____

5. _____

6. _____

7. _____

8. _____

🔊 **Read**

This newspaper article discusses one issue in the debate about climate change.

Weather, Climate, or Both?

In the summer of 2010, parts of eastern and southern Europe baked in temperatures they had never experienced before. Ukraine
5 saw its highest temperature ever recorded—106.3 degrees Fahrenheit (41.3 degrees Celsius)—and the island of Cyprus recorded an air temperature of 115.9 degrees F
10 (46.6 degrees C). As the **core** of the heat moved over Russia, about 15,000 people died. Many people interpreted the brutal heat as evidence that the climate of Earth
15 really has changed, that the **phenomenon** known as global warming[1] has really set in.

In December 2010, several feet of snow fell in some **sections** of northern Europe
20 that normally get only a few inches all year. Several cities in Germany shivered through coldest-ever temperatures sometimes reaching –20 degrees Celsius (–4 degrees F). In 2011, New York City posted its snowiest
25 January on record, as the monthly snowfall total hit 36 inches (91.4 cm). The normal snowfall in the city for an entire year is 22.4 inches (56.9 cm). Many people interpreted the cold and snow as evidence
30 that Earth's climate could not possibly be getting warmer.

A LOGICAL PROBLEM

Two opposite conclusions were drawn, each with evidence that was recent and easily observed by millions of people. Was Earth's
35 climate getting warmer or not? Which conclusion was right? Actually, neither. The unusual heat and cold observed in 2010 and 2011 are striking, but by themselves they indicate nothing about long-term processes such
40 as global warming. The logic is faulty because it treats two separate **phenomena**, weather and climate, as if they were the same thing.

Bermuda High off the U.S. coast

Weather is what happens in the short term—day to day, week to week. It's today's rain
45 or tomorrow's sunshine or the strong wind that messes up your hair. Climate **exhibits** itself over much longer periods. Weather indicates climate, but only if observed long enough to tell a **coherent** tale. A weather pattern that occurs in
50 40 years out of 50 may start scientists suspecting[2] a climate change. The scientists— or their grandchildren—would feel a lot more confident announcing climate change if the pattern held for 80 years out of 100.
55 Of course, climate determines what weather is normal. Consider the "Bermuda High" that

---

[1] *global warming:* a process by which Earth's overall average temperatures are rising
[2] *suspecting:* thinking—but not being entirely sure—that a bad thing is true

establishes itself over the Atlantic Ocean each summer. This qualifies as a climate feature because there is long-standing evidence of it,
60 and it influences the weather over a very large region for a very long time. A strong Bermuda High has many effects on weather. For one thing, it **ensures** that hot and humid air flows over the southeastern United States and even
65 reaches more northerly cities like Washington, D.C. For another, a strong Bermuda High steers the **energy** of many July and August storms northward along the U.S. Atlantic coast instead of westward to the Gulf of Mexico.
70 Meteorologists trying to guess where a hurricane may go are likely to check the strength of this climate feature before making predictions.

CLIMATE CHANGE AND HISTORY

Climate change can have huge effects. In ancient Rome, North Africa was known as "the
75 **granary**[3] of the empire," providing much of the Romans' wheat and other basic foods. Then, in about 100 BCE, the North African climate became far drier than in **previous** times, limiting farming to a few narrow strips beside
80 the Mediterranean Sea. In northern Europe the **interval** from about 950 CE to 1250 CE, known as the Medieval Warm Period, altered civilizations. Ice in the North Atlantic Ocean melted enough to clear new sailing **routes**, and

85 the Vikings of Denmark and Norway took advantage of the change. They settled Iceland, established farm communities in southwest Greenland, and even sailed to what is now Canada. Then, in the late 1200s, northern
90 Europe's climate changed again, becoming much cooler. Vikings could no longer sail ice-free seas from Europe to **assist** their Greenland colony, which gradually died off. Iceland remained inhabited, but life was much
95 harder than during the warm period.

Climatologists keep trying to develop a **strategy** for detecting climate changes without waiting a hundred years. They've run weather data through some of the world's most powerful
100 computers. Some of their models say that a warmer Earth would see greater extremes— hotter summers and colder winters and more vicious storms year-round. But when Cyprus broils or New York City gets buried in snow,
105 is that an example of what the models predict? No one really knows. The fact that all of the Earth's ten hottest years on record have occurred since 1998 easily **reinforces** the belief that Earth's climate is warming. Then again,
110 climatologists say that even this impressive statistic could just be a coincidence. Climate change is clearly visible only in hindsight, after it has already occurred. ■

---

[3] *granary:* a place where grain, such as wheat or corn, is stored

Reading Comprehension

Mark each sentence as *T* (true) or *F* (false) according to the information in Reading 2. Use the dictionary to help you understand new words.

___ 1. Europe's summer heat in 2010 shows that Earth's climate is certainly warming.

___ 2. In 2011, New York City had more snow in a month than it normally has in a whole year.

___ 3. The unusual heat and cold in 2010 and 2011 are climate phenomena, not weather.

___ 4. Weather is measured over longer time periods than climate is.

___ 5. The Bermuda High is classified as a climate feature partly because it has appeared almost every year for a long time.

___ 6. Because of climate change, North Africa is less suitable for farming now than in the days of the Roman Empire.

___ 7. The Medieval Warm Period prevented the Vikings from reaching their colony in Greenland.

____ 8. In about 950 CE and about 1250 CE, weather changed but climate did not.

____ 9. Because all of the Earth's ten hottest years have been since 1998, scientists are now sure that a climate change has occurred.

____10. Climate change is nearly impossible to recognize until after it has happened.

READING SKILL Reading Charts and Graphs

APPLY

A biome is a type of environment that supports certain living things. Biomes are often identified by the types of plants that dominate in the area. For example, a deciduous forest biome is dominated by trees that lose their leaves in winter. Climate is crucial to the formation of biomes.

Description / climate of selected biomes			
Biome	Description	Typical annual temperature range (degrees Fahrenheit)	Typical annual precipitation (inches)
Deciduous forest, (e.g., eastern U.S.)	Trees are oak, maple, beech, and other hardwoods. Four observable seasons: winter, spring, summer, and fall. Most trees lose their leaves in winter.	–22 to 86	between 29 and 59
Desert (e.g., Egypt)	Very dry. Large difference between day and night temperatures. Mostly in zones of falling air between 18 degrees and 28 degrees latitude, both north and south.	25 to 100	about 10
Grassland (e.g., Argentina; Southern Hemisphere)	Open, continuous grass and low-growing wildflowers over wide areas; generally flat. Rainfall is too low to support many trees. Soil beneath grass is often fertile.	–4 to 86	between 20 and 35
Rainforest (e.g., Belize)	Tropical rainforests are hot and moist all year. Temperate rainforests are cool and humid. No frost or freezes. High, broad canopy of leaves limits sunlight reaching the ground. Relatively few ground-level plants.	68 to 92	between 79 and 394
Shrubland (e.g., South Africa; Southern Hemisphere)	Usually on hilly, intermittently rocky ground on Western coasts of continents between 30 degrees and 40 degrees latitude, north and south. Small trees and aromatic herbs.	varies widely by elevation; range of –20 to 100 at about 500 feet of elevation	between 8 and 39
Tundra (e.g., Russia)	Bitterly cold in winter. Little rain year-round, but soil remains moist because of low evaporation. Most of the soil, except for the top 6 inches or so, stays frozen. Few trees or shrubs. Mostly moss, lichens, and low tufts of grass.	–40 to 64	between 6 and 10

A. Using the information in the chart above, answer the following questions in your notebook.

1. Which biome has the widest range of temperatures? Which has the smallest range?

2. Which two biomes are the driest?

3. From the data in this chart, which two biomes are found between specific latitudes on Earth?

4. In your opinion, which biome would be the nicest to visit? Why?

B. Next, write three questions to ask a partner, based on the chart.

Vocabulary Activities | STEP I: Word Level

A. Complete the sentences about "thundersnow" using the target vocabulary in the box. Use each item one time. Use the synonyms in parentheses to help you.

disoriented	exhibit	reinforces
energy	phenomenon	section

1. One Saturday morning in March 1993, many people in the eastern United States woke up to the sounds of high winds and crashing thunder. They were _____ by what they heard, and they ran to their windows to see
(confused)
flashes of light amidst heavy, blowing snow. Thunder and lightning during a blizzard?

2. Most snowstorms do not produce thunder and lightning because there is not enough _____ in the atmosphere.
(power)

3. Although it is an unusual occurrence, thunderstorms can accompany a snowstorm. This weather _____ is known as *thundersnow*.
(happening)

4. The troposphere is the _____ of the atmosphere closest to
(part)
Earth's surface. An extremely powerful winter storm system, if accompanied by intensely cold air in the upper regions of the troposphere, can produce thundersnow.

5. Although thundersnow is uncommon in most parts of the world, storms in the Great Lakes region of the northern United States and Canada do _____ it.
(display)

6. Thundersnow also occurs around the Rocky Mountains of western North America, particularly during the spring and fall. The great height of the western slopes of the mountains _____ the rising air.
(strengthens)

B. Many academic words are also considered formal words. Which of the target words in this unit (see the chart on page 65) are more formal synonyms for these informal words? Be sure to use the right forms of the target words.

Informal	Formal
1. earlier	_____
2. show	_____
3. strengthen	_____
4. way	_____
5. main	_____
6. break (time period)	_____

C. Read the sample sentences that feature forms of the word *orient*. Then answer the questions below in your notebook, using a dictionary as suggested. Compare answers with a partner.

> a. Before the school year starts, new students attend a one-day **orientation**.
> b. After getting off the roller coaster, Andrea felt dizzy and **disoriented**.
> c. Keep heading north. If you get confused, that bright star can **orient** you.
> d. Children can attend the workshop, but it's really more adult **oriented**.

1. Check (✓) the word closest in meaning to *orient*. Consult your dictionary before you answer.

   ___ direct   ___ configure   ___ expose   ___ mentor

2. Match the form of *orient* in each sentence with one of the meanings below.

confused	informational meeting	point in the right direction	suitable

   a. _____   c. _____

   b. _____   d. _____

3. Look at the sample sentences in your dictionary for *orient* and its forms. Who or what is being oriented or disoriented in each of those samples?

4. Does *orient* have any forms that are not used in the sample sentences in the box above? If so, what are they? Consult your dictionary.

Vocabulary Activities   STEP II: Sentence Level

The adjective *coherent* refers to things fitting together in a logical order, or being clear and easy to understand. The noun is *coherence*.

> *The police have a **coherent** plan in place for rescuing people after a snowstorm.*

To indicate the opposite, you can say that something is *incoherent* or that it *lacks coherence*.

> *His essay on gamma rays has a lot of good information, but it lacks **coherence**.*

CORPUS

D. Check the things for which coherence is very important. Then write a few sentences in your notebook for each item explaining why coherence is or is not important. Discuss your choices in a small group. Refer to your explanations when you argue your point.

___ 1. a children's storybook   ___ 5. city streets

___ 2. directions to a business   ___ 6. a friend's story about her vacation

___ 3. a painting   ___ 7. the arrangement of items in a grocery store

___ 4. the way you study for a test   ___ 8. music

The verb *exhibit* means "to show something to the public." The noun forms in this context are *exhibition* and *exhibitor.*

> The people who were rescued **exhibited** signs of disorientation.

> She **exhibited** her paintings in the New Artists **Exhibition** downtown, which had more than 100 **exhibitors** in all.

In legal proceedings, such as trials and lawsuits, the pieces of physical evidence that each side presents are referred to as *exhibits.*

> The lawyer for the defense presented the broken fencepost as **Exhibit** A.
> He entered about twenty **exhibits** into evidence.

CORPUS

E. You are the lawyer for the defense. Read the summary of the facts in this case and answer the questions that follow on this and the next page.

  Case summary: Your client, Mr. Logan, was driving home from work. While en route, a snowstorm started and he became disoriented. He drove into the yard of a neighbor, Mr. Simms, and knocked down his fence. Mr. Logan continued back to the road and went home. The next day, he went to Mr. Simms and explained what happened. Logan assisted Mr. Simms in repairing the fence and even reinforced it to ensure that it would be strong all winter. He paid for all materials. Two months later, Mr. Simms's lawyer called your client to tell him that Simms was suing him for $5,000.00. Simms claims that repairing the fence is not enough. His yard will need work in the spring, which Logan should pay for, and Logan should be punished for his bad driving.

1. What strategy will you use in this case?

   a. Prove Mr. Logan is an excellent driver. This is one minor mistake that he has done his best to correct. He should not be punished in any way.

   b. Present Mr. Logan as an equal victim in this situation. Both parties suffered because of weather phenomena that they could not control.

   c. Paint Mr. Simms as a greedy man who is only trying to get money from Mr. Logan.

   d. Argue that the interval between accident and claim was too long. Any claim against any person should be made in a timely manner. If the judge allows this, then anyone who ever made a mistake could be sued at any time in his or her life, which is unfair.

   e. Other: _____

2. List three points you would make to support your argument.

a. _____

b. _____

c. _____

3. What evidence could you use to support each point?

a. _____

b. _____

c. _____

4. What exhibits (physical things, pictures, or documents) will you present to support your argument? Make a list in your notebook.

5. How will you argue your case to the judge? Bring all the points and evidence together into one coherent argument (a summary of your case). Write your argument to the judge in your notebook.

F. Read the argument you prepared in activity E to a partner to make sure it is coherent. Revise your argument according to your partner's feedback. Then read your argument aloud in class. Your classmates will act as the jury and vote on your case.

G. Self-Assessment Review: Go back to page 65 and reassess your knowledge of the target vocabulary. How has your understanding of the words changed? What words do you feel most comfortable with now?

Writing and Discussion Topics

Write about or discuss the following topics.

1. Most forensic meteorologists are private parties who sell their services. One side or another hires the meteorologist to say certain things in court. What are some problems that may result?

2. The availability of weather data via the Internet raises the question, "Are forensic meteorologists really necessary?" What do you think? Give reasons for your opinion.

3. Many types of weather can be dangerous. Choose a weather phenomenon and do some Internet research about it. Explain why it is dangerous.

UNIT 6

Brain Food

In this unit, you will

> read about some ways that food can affect psychological and cognitive functions.
> review scanning.
> increase your understanding of the target academic words for this unit.

READING SKILL Summarizing

Self-Assessment

Think about how well you know each target word, and check (✓) the appropriate column. I have…

TARGET WORDS	never seen the word before	seen the word but am not sure what it means	seen the word and understand what it means	used the word, but am not sure if correctly	used the word confidently in *either* speaking *or* writing	used the word confidently in *both* speaking *and* writing
AWL						
🔑 affect						
allocate						
🔑 commit						
compile						
coordinate						
discrete						
journal						
🔑 mental						
🔑 overall						
paradigm						
🔑 period						
🔑 promote						
🔑 prospect						
🔑 react						
🔑 team						

🔑 Oxford 3000™ keywords

 Outside the Reading What do you know about nutrition? Watch the video on the student website to find out more.

Before You Read

Read these questions. Discuss your answers in a small group.

1. Name three or four foods you often eat even though you know they're not good for you. Why are they unhealthful? Why do you eat them anyway?

2. Name three or four foods you eat that are healthful. Why are they healthful? Do you like the way they taste?

3. Have you ever felt a significant improvement in your mood or in your concentration after a meal or snack? What do you think caused this effect?

MORE WORDS YOU'LL NEED

cognitive: related to thought and learning

diet: the set of foods a person usually eats

intolerant: unwilling or unable to accept certain behavior or circumstances

Read

This excerpt from a nutrition manual explains the psychological benefits of eating certain fats.

FAT FOR BRAINS

As the old saying goes, you are what you eat. The foods you eat obviously **affect** your body's performance. They may also influence how your brain handles its
5 tasks. If it handles them well, you think more clearly, and you are more emotionally stable. The right foods can help you concentrate, keep you motivated, sharpen your memory, speed your **reaction** time, reduce stress, and perhaps
10 even prevent brain aging.

GOOD AND BAD FAT

Most people associate the term *fat* with poor health. We are encouraged to eat fat-free foods and to drain fat away from fried foods. To understand its nutritional benefits, however, we
15 have to change the **paradigm** for how we think about fat.

The first step is gaining a better understanding of fat. Instead of conceiving of it as a single thing, we have to recognize it as several
20 **discrete** types of a similar compound. Not every fat is your enemy. Fats—the right kinds and in the right amounts—are among your best friends. It is smart to **commit** to a balanced-fat diet, not to a no-fat diet.

Foods high in saturated fats

Foods high in unsaturated fats

Fats are broadly classified as either "saturated" or "unsaturated." Most foods that contain fat contain both kinds, in varying proportions. Foods that are high in saturated fats include meat, butter, and other animal products. In general, saturated fats are solid at room temperature. Foods high in unsaturated fats include vegetable oils, nuts, and avocados. Unsaturated fats, if separated out, are usually liquid at room temperature.

The key to health is to **allocate** a percentage of your fat intake to each type of fat. Saturated fat in moderate amounts poses no problem. In general, you will be fine if less than 20 percent of the fat you consume is saturated. Beyond that level, saturated fat may **promote** heart disease and perhaps some types of cancer. A diet high in saturated fat can also make you depressed and antisocial, and impair your general **mental** performance. Unsaturated fats should make up most of your fat intake. But beware. Unsaturated fats are especially high in calories and could cause weight problems. The smart approach is to keep your **overall** fat intake low and make sure that most of it is in the form of unsaturated fats.

FATTY ACIDS

Keeping your fat intake too low, on the other hand, could also be dangerous. Fat in food is broken down into chemicals called fatty acids. The body uses them for many purposes. They go into all hormones[1]. They are critical to body metabolism[2]. And they are part of the outer membrane[3] of every cell in the body, including those in the brain. You need these fatty acids in order to stay physically healthy and **mentally** sharp.

Of the many fatty acids the body uses, two are called "essential fatty acids" (EFAs). Your diet must contain foods that provide them, because the body cannot make them on its own. The most important are omega-3 fatty acids. They are crucial for the proper development of the human brain. All brain-cell membranes need to refresh themselves continually with new supplies of omega-3s.

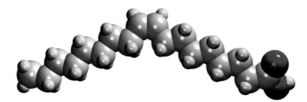
The structure of oleic acid, an omega-3 fatty acid

North Americans are famous for consuming too much saturated fat and too much total fat. They also consume far too little food that provides omega-3s. The vegetable oils most commonly used in cooking—corn, safflower, and sunflower oils—have almost no omega-3s.

Using canola (rapeseed), soy, and walnut oils, which contain a lot of omega-3s, would be far more healthful. A diet with a lot of olive oil, such as the traditional diets of Italy, Greece, and other Mediterranean regions, would also be better. And the old saying about fish being brain food is true. Fatty fish that live in cold water—such as salmon, tuna, and herring—are rich in omega-3s, especially in one called DHA. It is identical to a material in human nerve cells. Even if you don't eat fish, you can still get the DHA you need from green vegetables, sesame seeds, and egg yolks.

OMEGA-3S AND THE BRAIN

There is evidence that DHA plays a big role in the intellectual development of humans. In one study, doctors measured the DHA levels of mothers at the time they gave birth. Their children were then tested at 12 and 18 months of age to see how well they paid attention to things around them. The research **team** **compiled** data on how long each child focused on a toy. The toddlers whose mothers had the highest DHA levels at birth showed the greatest attention spans. These children focused for longer **periods** and spent much less time simply looking around, unfocused.

In psychology and physiology **journals**, articles routinely confirm the value of omega-3 fatty acids. One published study demonstrated that fish oil reduced the degree of brain damage in cats experiencing stroke. A study by

[1] *hormones:* chemicals that control body processes such as growth
[2] *metabolism:* the body process that changes food into chemicals the body needs
[3] *membrane:* a thin covering around a cell or larger body part

researchers at the University of Pittsburgh showed that adults with low levels of omega-3s in their bodies were far more depressed, pessimistic, and impulsive than those with normal or high levels. This evidence improves the **prospects** for treating depressed patients effectively. Many therapists now say they are determined to **coordinate** psychological therapy with dietary therapy in order to rely less on drugs.

As research continues to show, new ways of thinking about fat can open the door to better physical, **mental,** and emotional health. ■

Reading Comprehension

Mark each sentence as *T* (true) or *F* (false) according to the information in Reading 1. Use the dictionary to help you understand new words.

___ 1. Foods affect a person's moods and motivation.

___ 2. Ideally, more people should commit to no-fat diets.

___ 3. At room temperature, you could pour unsaturated fat out of a bottle.

___ 4. It is not healthful to eat a very large amount of unsaturated fat.

___ 5. Omega-3 fatty acids promote intellectual development.

___ 6. A study showed that children born from high-DHA mothers are better able to pay attention.

___ 7. Research journals reported that people with a lot of omega-3 fats in their systems were very depressed.

___ 8. Patients with psychological problems should coordinate their therapy so that it includes dietary as well as psychological treatment.

READING SKILL   Summarizing

LEARN

A summary of a reading text should be short. It should cover all the main ideas and give an overall idea of the text. It may include some important supporting points, but it should NOT emphasize smaller points. Think of a summary as an outline or a graphic organizer in paragraph form (see Unit 4 for more on outlining).

The best summaries come from a good understanding of the whole reading. There are, however, some techniques that can help you prepare a good summary:

- State the main idea of the whole text in your first sentence.

- Look at headings to help you identify some of the main ideas.

- Scan paragraphs to identify their topics. Do not simply look for "topic sentences." Not every paragraph has one, and those that exist are not always easy to locate.

- For each main point, add one reason from the text that explains why it is important.

APPLY

A. Use the headings in Reading 1 and any obvious paragraph clues to decide whether each of these topics belongs in a summary of the reading. Check (✓) the items that should be included. Discuss your choices with a partner.

___ a balance of fats   ___ obesity

___ brain cells   ___ omega-3s

___ canola oil   ___ psychological therapy

___ DHA   ___ saturated and unsaturated fats

___ fish   ___ the United States

___ IQ and depression   ___ the University of Pittsburgh

B. Complete the graphic organizer to show the structure of ideas in Reading 1.

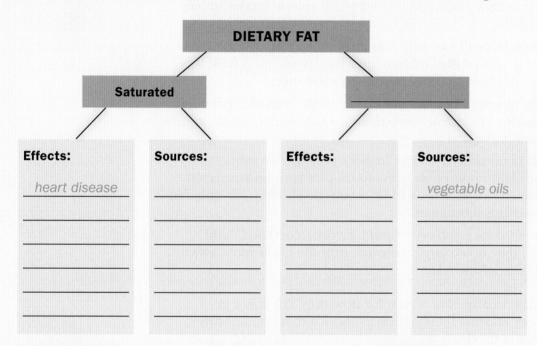

DIETARY FAT

Saturated

Effects:
heart disease
_____
_____
_____
_____
_____

Sources:
_____
_____
_____
_____
_____

Effects:
_____
_____
_____
_____
_____

Sources:
vegetable oils
_____
_____
_____
_____

C. Write a one-paragraph summary of Reading 1 using the main ideas and structure from the graphic organizer. Your summary should be no more than 80 words long.

REVIEW A SKILL Scanning (See p. 36)

Scan Reading 1 to find the answers to these questions. Before you begin, talk with a partner about what clues (e.g., capital letters or special puctuation) you will look for.

1. What two groups are fats classified into?

2. At the most, what percentage of the fats you consume should be saturated?

3. Which two countries are mentioned in the reading as having diets with a lot of olive oil?

Vocabulary Activities   STEP I: Word Level

A. Read these excerpts from another article on the psychological effects of food. In each excerpt, cross out the one word or phrase in parentheses with a different meaning from the other three choices. Compare answers with a partner.

1. Many studies have tried to determine whether Attention Deficit Hyperactivity Disorder (ADHD) is (*influenced / affected / caused / impacted*) by the foods children eat. The goal is to test claims that ADHD symptoms, like poor concentration and impulsive behavior, are triggered by something in food.

2. If they are, eliminating these "provoking substances" would presumably (*complete / encourage / promote / facilitate*) healthier behavior.

3. Some researchers have focused on diets that eliminate many food additives and even ban some foods. Others study "few-foods" diets—those that (*convert / divide / distribute / allocate*) a child's total calorie intake among only a few types of food.

4. One study found that, (*overall / in total / as a whole / finally*), behavior problems increased in 69% of the children after they were given food containing colorings or other possibly provoking substances.

5. In another study, the research (*team / sponsor / group / squad*) monitored brain activity by looking at electroencephalograms (EEGs), which are graphs of electrical impulses in the brain.

6. First, they recorded brain activity during (*times / periods / sections / intervals*) when the children were on a few-foods diet with no suspected provoking substances. Then they took EEGs when the children ate only foods with suspected provoking substances.

7. After the researchers (*wrote / gathered / put together / compiled*) and compared the EEGs, they noted large increases in some brain-wave activity during the second stage of the test.

People and organizations usually have a plan for how they are going to use their resources—they *allocate* their resources. Notice that you *allocate* something *to* or *for* something else.

> We **allocated** 20% of our budget to advertising.

The noun form is *allocation*, and the adjective is *allocable* (or *allocatable*).

> The highest priorities typically get the greatest **allocation** of resources.

> Some **allocable** resources are money, fuel, space, time, and attention.

CORPUS

B. During a typical week, how much time do you allocate to these activities (not how much time you spend doing them, but how much time you plan for them)? Estimate the time in hours. Compare answers with a partner.

1. watching TV   _____
2. hanging out with friends   _____
3. reading for pleasure   _____
4. playing video games   _____
5. going to the movies   _____
6. studying   _____
7. using the Internet   _____
8. playing team sports   _____

C. Check (✓) the activities that require you to coordinate with other people. Then decide what type of coordination is necessary (schedules, access, meeting times, etc.). Compare answers with a partner.

Activity	**Type of coordination**
___ 1. watching TV	_____
___ 2. hanging out with friends	_____
___ 3. reading for pleasure	_____
___ 4. playing video games	_____
___ 5. going to the movies	_____
___ 6. studying	_____
___ 7. using the Internet	_____
___ 8. playing team sports	_____

Word Form Chart			
Noun	**Verb**	**Adjective**	**Adverb**
commitment	commit	committed	_____

D. The word *commit* has several different meanings and uses, depending on context. Match each phrase with its example sentence. Then rewrite the example sentences using the matching phrase.

a. commit a crime

b. not commit yourself

c. be totally committed to someone

d. have a commitment

e. have commitments

f. honor a commitment

g. get out of a commitment

h. make a (financial) commitment to something

i. a lack of commitment

_i_ 1. I promised to give money every month to the Diabetes Research Foundation.

   I made a financial commitment to the Diabetes Research Foundation.

___ 2. I can't meet at that time because I've promised to do something else then.

_____

___ 3. All she thinks about is her daughter.

_____

___ 4. His leaving early shows that he doesn't care about this team enough.

_____

___ 5. The government has fulfilled the promise to allocate more money to the school lunches program.

_____

___ 6. He went to prison for carrying out several illegal acts.

_____

___ 7. She thinks she can come tomorrow, but she won't promise until she talks to her sister.

_____

___ 8. They would love to take a vacation, but they have responsibilities that need their attention.

_____

___ 9. He's not really sick. He's just trying to avoid keeping a promise he made.

_____

Word Form Chart			
Noun	**Verb**	**Adjective**	**Adverb**
_____	affect	affected unaffected	_____
mentality	_____	mental	mentally
_____	_____	overall	overall
promotion promoter	promote	promotional	promotionally
prospect prospects	_____	prospective	prospectively
reaction	react	reactive	_____

E. Read more information about how diet affects cognitive functioning. Then restate the information in your notebook, using the word(s) in parentheses. Be prepared to read aloud or discuss your sentences in class.

1. Chemicals in your diet called antioxidants may influence your mental functions more strongly as you grow older. (*affect*)

   *Dietary chemicals called antioxidants may **affect** your thinking more strongly as you get older.*

2. A number of studies have suggested that antioxidants help maintain memory skills and other cognitive functions in older adults. (*mentally*)

3. By going through certain chemical processes, antioxidants limit the damage that some harmful chemicals called "free radicals" can do. (*react* or *reaction*)

4. Free radicals cause damage to tissues in nearly every part of the body. Their general effect on the body is partly responsible for the slow decline we call "aging." (*overall, promote*)

5. One of the most disturbing aspects of aging is what happens to the brain. Aging can cause slower reaction times, memory loss, and a dulling of the senses. (*affect*)

6. Some people seem to have improved their chances of staying sharp in old age by eating foods that contain adequate amounts of antioxidants. (*prospects*)

7. It seems, however, that the form of antioxidants matters. In several studies, older people who took antioxidants in the form of pills showed no improvement. (*unaffected*)

Before You Read

Read these questions. Discuss your answers in a small group.

1. War often causes widespread hunger. Why does this happen?

2. Have you ever seen someone suffering from long-term undernourishment, perhaps because of poverty or disease? Have you ever seen a picture of such a person? Describe the way he or she looked.

3. Have you ever been very hungry or very thirsty? How did that affect your mood? Did it affect your ability to think? How?

Read

This excerpt from a nutrition textbook tells the story of the first clinical study of the effects of starvation on physical and mental functioning.

The Minnesota Starvation Experiment

On November 19, 1944, 40 healthy young men entered the Laboratory of Physiological Hygiene at the University of Minnesota. They were ready to embark on a grueling medical experiment.
5 The men had responded to a brochure that asked: "Will You Starve That They Be Better Fed?" World War II was coming to a close, and the Allied forces[1] needed to know how to deal with starving people in areas of Europe and
10 Asia ruined by the war.

BASIC DESIGN

In 1944, the **prospect** of finding healthy young men to volunteer for such an experiment was dim. Many were overseas serving in the military. However, many conscientious
15 objectors—those who refused to serve in the war for religious or moral reasons—remained in the United States doing various types of community service. The government eventually allowed them to volunteer for medical
20 experiments. About 400 men volunteered for the Minnesota research, of whom 40 were eventually selected.

The study took place in
25 three **discrete** stages. The first, starting in November 1944, was a
30 "standardization" **period** of 3 months. So they could be observed under non-stressful
35 conditions, the men received a substantial 3,200 calories of food per day. This was
40 followed by a 6-month semi-starvation **period,** beginning on February 12, 1945, in which they received only 1,800 calories per day. The semi-starvation diet reflected what was available in the war-torn
45 areas of Europe—potatoes, turnips, rutabagas, dark bread, and macaroni. The final 3 months

Cover of a brochure for the Minnesota Starvation Experiment

---

[1] *Allied forces:* the group of nations working together in World War II consisting primarily of the United States, the United Kingdom, the Soviet Union, and China

were a nutritional rehabilitation **period.**

Throughout the study, participants were given various housekeeping and administrative duties within the laboratory. They were also allowed to participate in university classes and activities. The participants were expected to walk 22 miles (35.4 kilometers) per week and to expend 3,009 calories per day.

THE GOOD DAYS

Those selected to participate were a well-educated group. All had completed some college coursework. Many took advantage of the opportunity to take more courses at the University of Minnesota during the experiment. Initially, their blue pants, white shirts, and sturdy walking shoes were all that distinguished them from other people on campus. During the standardization **period,** the men felt well-fed and full of energy.

Many initially volunteered for local charities, participated in music and drama productions, or otherwise contributed to community projects in the area.

Participants in the Minnesota Starvation Experiment

SEMI-STARVATION

On the first day of semi-starvation (February 12, 1945), the men sat down to a meal that included a small bowl of hot cereal, two slices of toast, a dish of fried potatoes, a dish of Jello, a small portion of jam, and a small glass of milk. Each was now **allocated** less than half the calories he was used to consuming. The men ate their meals together in Shevlin Hall on the campus. Participants were supposed to lose

2.5 pounds (1.1 kg) per week to reach the desired 25% weight reduction by the end of the semi-starvation **period.**

As semi-starvation progressed, the men became irritable and intolerant of one another. Many of them kept **journals** during the experiment, which recorded their feelings and **reactions** as they happened. One of the men, Carlyle Frederick, later remembered "noticing what's wrong with everybody else, even your best friend. Little things that wouldn't bother me before or after would really make me upset." Another, Marshall Sutton, noted, "We were impatient waiting in line if we had to, and we'd get disturbed with each other's eating habits at times. We became, in a sense, more introverted[2], and we had less energy." The men reported feeling cold much of the time and asked for extra blankets even in the middle of summer. They experienced dizziness, extreme tiredness, muscle soreness, hair loss, reduced **coordination,** and ringing in their ears. They felt weak **mentally** as well as physically. Several were forced to quit their university classes because they simply didn't have the energy or motivation to attend and concentrate. Food became an obsession.

The men became more noticeable around campus as they began to show visible signs of starvation—sunken faces and bellies, protruding ribs, and swollen legs, ankles, and faces. Despite the challenges of starvation, there was a determination among the men that somehow kept them **committed.** When each of the 36 men who completed the experiment was asked if he had ever considered withdrawing, the reply was repeatedly firm and succinct: "No."

SLOW RECOVERY

The three-month rehabilitation **period** began at the end of July 1945 and continued until October 20, 1945. With the end of the war that summer, the results of the experiment were becoming increasingly relevant. How can the winners of the war best **promote** the recovery of starving populations in Europe and Asia? As the experiment showed, the answer was far more complex than simply, "Give them food."

---

[2] *introverted:* quiet and shy, concerned only with one's own thoughts and feelings

Many of the men reported that, **overall,** the
125 rehabilitation **period** was the hardest of all.
Their strength came back only slowly, and
many were depressed by this delayed recovery.
Their feelings of hunger remained. They
continued to be dizzy, confused, and irritable.
130 The research **team** eventually **compiled** and
published these results in academic **journals.**

They also prepared a relief worker's manual that
focused on the psychological effects of food
135 deprivation. The experiment helped create a
new **paradigm** for understanding starvation.
Previously, starvation was seen as only a
physical thing. The experiment showed that it
dramatically alters personality and that nutrition
140 directly and predictably **affects** the mind. ■

Reading Comprehension

Mark each sentence as *T* (true) or *F* (false) according to the information in Reading 2.
Use the dictionary to help you understand new words.

___ 1. The Minnesota Starvation Experiment involved soldiers from the Allied
Forces.

___ 2. The experiment compiled data to help deal with starvation problems in
Europe and Asia.

___ 3. In the first stage of the experiment, the men ate so much they became
obese.

___ 4. In the second stage of the experiment, the men continued walking 22 miles
per week.

___ 5. In the third stage of the experiment, the men quickly regained their
previous health.

___ 6. The men's journals record that they became depressed and irritable as they
began to lose weight.

___ 7. Eventually, the participants lost all mental motivation to continue in the
experiment.

___ 8. The study showed that rehabilitating starved populations involved more
than food supplies.

READING SKILL
Summarizing

APPLY

A. Using subheadings and paragraph clues, plan a 100-word summary of Reading 2. Outline your plan below, but do not write the summary yet. Discuss your plan with a partner.

_____

_____

_____

_____

B. Keeping in mind your partner's comments, revise your plan. Then write a 100-word summary of Reading 2 in your notebook.

Vocabulary Activities | STEP I: Word Level

A. Many academic words are also considered formal words. Which of the target words in this unit (see the chart on page 81) are more formal synonyms for these informal words? Be sure to use the right forms of the target words.

Informal	Formal
1. length of time	_____
2. put together	_____
3. magazine	_____
4. set aside	_____
5. separate	_____
6. push	_____

B. Complete the sentences about nutrition and child development using the target vocabulary in the box. Use each item one time. Use the synonyms in parentheses to help you. (Note: The sentences are not yet in the correct order.)

affect	mental	paradigm	prospect
compiled	overall	promote	reacted
coordination			

___ a. At the other end of the weight spectrum, obesity may negatively

  _____ a child's image of himself or herself. This may lead to
  (have an impact on)
  lower academic performance for overweight children.

___ b. Data _____ by government agencies suggest that providing
         (gathered together)
  breakfast to school-age children has lessened these problems.

___ c. Nutritionists use the term *food-insecure* to mean "not sure whether healthy

  meals will be consistently available." By emphasizing a child's attitudes

  and expectations instead of actual food intake, this reflects a change in the

  current _____ among experts.
          (way of thinking)

___ d. One study showed that children in food-insecure households scored lower

  on mathematics tests, were more likely to have repeated a grade, and

  _____ more violently when teased by other children.
     (responded)

___ e. Other studies have found that child hunger raises the _____ of
                                                              (possibility)
  severe behavior problems and long-term anxiety/depression.

___ f. Overweight children are often slower than others in developing physical

  _____ and stamina. Because they cannot keep up with others
     (integrated movement)
  at play, they are more likely to be socially isolated than children who are

  not overweight.

___ g. Some schools reportedly have tried to _____ better test scores
                                              (increase the chances of)
  for the school _____ by providing healthier school lunches.
                  (as a whole)

___ h. Under-nutrition in children probably affects their _____
                                                          (related to the mind)
  development. Presumably, a lack of food deprives the brain of essential

  nutrients. Also, difficulties involving food probably have emotional

  consequences.

C. Put the sentences in activity B into a logical order to describe some effects of nutrition on child development. (More than one order may be possible.) Read your sequence to a partner.

D. Read the sample sentences that feature forms of the word *coordinate*. Then answer the questions below in your notebook, using a dictionary as suggested. Compare answers with a partner.

> a. The school superintendent **coordinates** the operations of 12 schools.
> b. Members of the choir are required to wear color-**coordinated** outfits for performances.
> c. Bad nutrition can affect a person's hand–eye **coordination**, making it difficult to play sports or music instruments.
> d. The camp hired an athletic **coordinator** to run its sports programs.

1. Check (✓) the word closest in meaning to *coordinate*. Consult your dictionary before you answer.

___ command

___ organize

___ reminisce

___ recur

2. Each of these sentences indicates that things were coordinated. What are they?

a. _____

b. _____

c. _____

d. _____

3. Look at the sample sentences in your dictionary for *coordinate* and its forms. What is being coordinated in each of those samples?

4. Does *coordinate* have any forms that are not used in the sample sentences in the box above? If so, what are they? Consult your dictionary.

Vocabulary Activities STEP II: Sentence Level

The adjective *discrete* describes something that is separate from or independent of other things of the same type. The adverb form is *discretely*.

> Fats can be divided into **discrete** types.

Note the spelling of *discrete*, and do not confuse it with another adjective, *discreet*, which means "careful not to attract attention and cause embarrassment."

CORPUS

E. Rewrite each of these sentences in your notebook, using *discrete* or *discretely*. Then go on to provide the information introduced in each sentence. Compare results with a partner.

1. A person's life can be divided into a few significant time periods.

2. A college career usually follows a series of levels.

3. Sometimes job responsibilities can include many highly varied tasks.

4. The Minnesota Starvation Experiment was broken into three distinct stages.

5. The people in my life promote my health and well-being in different ways.

Many medical and psychological experiments like the Minnesota Starvation Experiment are controversial and cause strong reactions both for and against them. Critics say that some of them are cruel, immoral, or mentally and physically harmful. Defenders of these experiments say they are necessary and justifiable because the knowledge they provide helps everyone.

F. Read this summary of an actual psychological experiment. What are the two most extreme reactions (for and against) that you can imagine? What is your own reaction? Do you think the experiment was justified? Why or why not? Write a one-paragraph summary in your notebook of the reactions you have listed. Be prepared to read aloud and discuss your work in a small group.

Experiment: In a 1971 psychology experiment, some college students were assigned to be "prisoners" and another group were assigned to be "guards." After only about a day, the "guards" started treating the "prisoners" cruelly. The guards admitted later that they began thinking of the prisoners as inferior. Some prisoners became frightened and tried to leave the experiment. The researchers said no. These prisoners felt trapped, depressed, and hopeless, just as real-life prisoners often do. In the end, the experiment—which was supposed to last several weeks—was canceled after only a few days. The researchers feared that someone might suffer serious physical or psychological harm.

G. Self-Assessment Review: Go back to page 81 and reassess your knowledge of the target vocabulary. How has your understanding of the words changed? What words do you feel most comfortable with now?

Writing and Discussion Topics

Write about or discuss the following topics.

1. When designing a diet for yourself or another person, what information would you need? How would you gather the data? How would you compile it? Are there any paradigms you would follow?

2. Cognitive and emotional difficulties are often partly caused by—or made worse by—an inadequate diet. ADHD is one such difficulty. What other illnesses or disorders can result from poor nutrition? Go online to research this topic, then present a summary of your results.

3. What are you committed to in your life? Describe your personal commitments and explain why you made these commitments.

UNIT 7

Roving Continents

In this unit, you will

> learn how scientific discovery led to our current knowledge of the movement of Earth's outer layer, the crust.
> read about exciting changes in the earth's crust in one part of the world.
> increase your understanding of the target academic words for this unit.

READING SKILL Making Inferences

Self-Assessment

Think about how well you know each target word, and check (✓) the appropriate column. I have...

TARGET WORDS	never seen the word before	seen the word but am not sure what it means	seen the word and understand what it means	used the word, but am not sure if correctly	used the word confidently in *either* speaking *or* writing	used the word confidently in *both* speaking *and* writing
AWL						
accommodate						
🔑 aid						
🔑 community						
comprehensive						
displace						
evolve						
fluctuate						
integrate						
intermediate						
🔑 nuclear						
random						
restrain						
🔑 reverse						
rigid						
🔑 transform						

🔑 Oxford 3000™ keywords

Outside the Reading What do you know about geology?
Watch the video on the student website to find out more.

Before You Read

Read these questions. Discuss your answers in a small group.

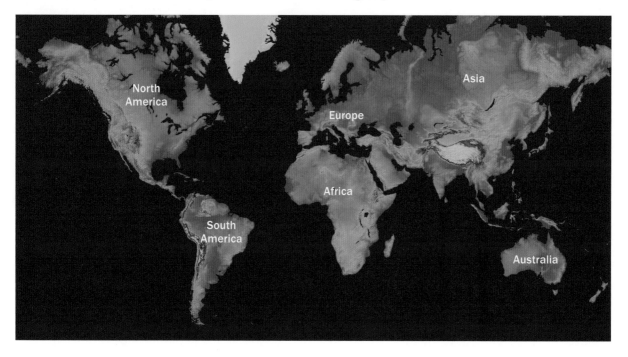

1. What continent do you live on now? Is it connected to other continents? Have you ever lived on (or visited) another continent?

2. Have scientists discovered any evidence that the climate on your continent was once very different from what it is now? What caused the change(s)?

3. Name two parts of the world that experience a lot of volcanic eruptions or earthquakes. What do you think causes these events?

MORE WORDS YOU'LL NEED

continent: a large landmass; the seven continents are Africa, Antarctica, Asia, Australia, Europe, North America, and South America

theory: a systematic explanation of how something works

This introduction to a chapter in a geology textbook explains the basic ideas behind the theory of a long-ago supercontinent on Earth.

Pieces of a Puzzle: The Evidence for Pangaea

In geology, a *plate* is a large, **rigid** area of solid rock. The earth's surface is built of about 40 plates, called *tectonic plates*—some as large as continents and others only
5 a few hundred miles across. Modern geology has shown that these tectonic plates move in relation to each other. Such movement is possible because the plates float on top of the *mantle*, the layer of molten[1] rock between the
10 planet's outer crust and its dense **nucleus**, called the *core*. Even before this theory of *plate tectonics* became accepted, many in the geological **community** believed Earth's continents had moved during the history of the
15 planet. They were right, but their ideas faced great opposition.

SUDDEN EVENTS

Until the 1700s, most Europeans explained the origins of Earth's bodies of water and landmasses in terms of "catastrophism."
20 According to this explanation, a few sudden, violent events (catastrophes) periodically **transformed** Earth's surface. Then, a revival of science in Europe **restrained** the imaginations of geographers. Catastrophism was **displaced**
25 by "uniformitarianism," a term derived from the word *uniform*. According to this explanation, the forces we see shaping the earth now are the same forces that shaped it in the past. Since most of the processes we see are slow and
30 gradual, we assume that, for the most part, Earth's surface was shaped slowly and gradually.

The belief that continents have not always been in their present positions was common long before the 20th century. In 1596, the Dutch
35 mapmaker Abraham Ortelius suggested that the

Americas were "torn away from Europe and Africa . . . by earthquakes and floods." As evidence, he pointed out that, if you imagine putting Africa and South America together, they
40 would fit almost like two puzzle pieces. The big opening along Africa's western coast would easily **accommodate** the "hump" in South America's eastern coastline.

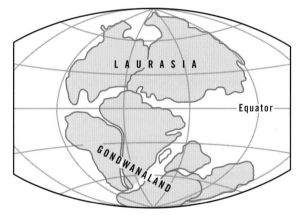
Pangaea splitting into Laurasia and Gondwanaland

WEGENER'S THEORY

More geologists began to think that the
45 arrangement of today's continents gradually **evolved**. In 1912, a scientific explanation, called the *theory of continental drift*, was proposed by a German meteorologist named Alfred Lothar Wegener. He argued that all of
50 Earth's landmasses were once joined in a single supercontinent, which he called *Pangaea* (from the Greek *pan-*, meaning "all" or "complete," and *Gaea*, meaning "Earth"). According to Wegener's theory, about 200 million years ago,
55 Pangaea began to split apart. One of Wegener's biggest supporters, Alexander Du Toit, proposed an **intermediate** stage. He said that

---

[1] *molten:* liquified due to heat; usually used to describe rock, such as volcanic lava

Evidence that Continents Were Once Joined		
Evidence	**Countries or Regions**	**Continents**
coal	Britain and the northeastern United States	Europe and North America
Glossopteris	throughout the Southern Hemisphere	Africa, Antarctica, Australia, South America
mountains	southern Africa and eastern Brazil	Africa and South America
red sandstone	northeastern Europe, Greenland, and Canada	Europe and North America
the shapes of continents	western Africa and eastern Brazil	Africa and South America

Pangaea first broke into two large continental landmasses: *Laurasia* in the northern
60 hemisphere and *Gondwanaland* in the south. Laurasia and Gondwanaland then continued to break apart into the various smaller continents that exist today.

Wegener's theory was based partly on the
65 remarkable fit of the South American and African continents noticed by Ortelius three centuries earlier. He and his supporters also offered other pieces of evidence. For example, fossils[2] of an ancient plant called *Glossopteris*
70 were found throughout the southern continents—Africa, Australia, Antarctica, and South America—and in India. If all these continents had not once been joined, *Glossopteris* would probably not have spread so
75 far. And if Antarctica had not once been closer to the equator, the plant would not have grown there at all.

Geological structures on today's separated continents also offered evidence. Some
80 mountains in South Africa are structurally similar to mountains in eastern Brazil. The coal deposits of Britain match deposits in the Appalachian Mountains of eastern North America. A band of red sandstone stretches
85 from northeastern Europe, through Greenland, and into Canada. These similarities seemed too numerous to be **random** coincidences.

BUT HOW?
Wegener's theory, especially his ideas about

Pangaea, took things too far for most of the
90 scientific **community.** They could accept uniform processes and a slow Africa/South America split, but not split after split and then long-distance travel by the continents. Their strongest objections centered on the question,
95 "How?" Some scientists tried to show that it was physically impossible for continental rock to move across the ocean floor. Such objections were entirely reasonable, and Wegener's theory had no good answer.

100 Finally, in the late 20th century, the theory of plate tectonics came to the **aid** of the theory of continental drift. It offered the **comprehensive** explanation of landmass movement that Wegener had been unable
105 to provide. New evidence made it hard to believe that the continents were *not* moving. The floor of the Atlantic Ocean was found to be spreading apart. New discoveries showed that the planet's magnetic field is not constant.
110 It **fluctuates** over very long time periods, and has clearly shifted several times. The theory's system of plates moving on molten rock offered a believable answer to the question, "How?" It **integrated** pieces of
115 evidence ranging from volcanic activity to the formation of mountains to the distribution of fossil plants. It shows that Pangaea not only could exist, but probably did. It also states that the trend toward separation will eventually
120 **reverse.** The continents will drift together again and form a new supercontinent. ■

---

[2] *fossils:* evidence, such as a piece of bone or a mark in a rock, left by an animal or plant that lived long ago

Reading Comprehension

Mark each sentence as *T* (true) or *F* (false) according to the information in Reading 1. Use the dictionary to help you understand new words.

___ 1. Earth's large landmasses continually move around the globe.

___ 2. Earth's crust is solid, but the other parts of the planet are liquid.

___ 3. Maps in the 1600s showed that Africa and South America might once have fit together.

___ 4. Alfred Wegener's theory was essentially the same as Ortelius's theory.

___ 5. *Glossopteris* fossils are widespread because the continents were once all at the equator.

___ 6. Some bands of rock appear on several separate continents.

___ 7. The biggest criticism of Wegener's theory was that it failed to explain the advantages of continental movement.

___ 8. The theory of plate tectonics solved the biggest problems posed by the theory of continental drift.

___ 9. Continents on either side of the Atlantic are moving away from each other.

___10. Someday, the continents might all be joined together again.

READING SKILL | Making Inferences

LEARN

When you make an inference, you use clues in a reading to understand something the author has not directly stated. The reading implies it, and you infer it. An inference is a conclusion that you draw from the information presented in the reading.

APPLY

Read the paragraph indicated again. Then select the one or two statements that can be most strongly inferred from each paragraph. Compare selections with a partner and explain your choices.

1. Paragraph 1:

   a. There are more small tectonic plates than large ones.

   b. The top layer of the mantle is liquid.

   c. The continents were formed from material in the mantle.

2. Paragraph 2:

   a. Catastrophists believed the earth should not change.

   b. Catastrophists believed that science was a bad thing.

   c. Catastrophists believed that forces observable today were not enough to shape the earth.

3. Paragraphs 4 and 5:

    a. Wegener formulated a theory about meteorology that also worked for geology.

    b. Wegener was not the only scientist of his time who thought Pangaea once existed.

    c. Wegener went on expeditions to explore the continents in the Southern Hemisphere.

4. Paragraph 7:

    a. Wegener's theory was weak in some respects.

    b. Wegener's opponents were all catastrophists.

    c. Wegener's opponents could not accept that a landmass might break into two.

Vocabulary Activities   STEP I: Word Level

A. Read these excerpts from an article on tectonic plates. For each excerpt, cross out the one word or phrase in parentheses with a different meaning from the other three choices. Compare answers with a partner.

1. *Geodesy* is the study of the size and shape of the earth. Over thousands of years, the tools of the field have (*fluctuated / developed / evolved / progressed*) so that now we can use geodetic measurements to track the movement of tectonic plates.

2. Because plate movements happen all over the globe at the same time, only satellite-based methods can give a truly (*all-inclusive / comprehensive / accurate / thorough*) view of them.

3. In the late 1970s, these space-based techniques completely (*improved / changed / altered / transformed*) the field of geodesy.

4. Of the space-based techniques, the Global Positioning System (GPS) has provided the most (*aid / assistance / truth / help*) to scientists studying the movements of Earth's crust.

5. By repeatedly measuring distances between specific points, geologists can determine if there has been significant (*displacement / restraint / movement / repositioning*) among the plates.

6. For example, scientists now know that earthquakes and volcanic eruptions along the lines between plates do not occur (*rigidly / by chance / randomly / haphazardly*).

7. Space-geodetic data have already confirmed that the present-day rates and directions of plate movement (*fit in / integrate / harmonize / evolve*) well with the geologists' estimates.

The word *integrate* means "to join things so that they become one thing or fit together." Often, sentences with *integrate* mention the individual things (or people) and the larger thing that eventually includes them.

> His theory **integrated** the work of several scientists in different fields of study.

> The new students slowly **integrated** into the social groups on campus.

CORPUS

B. What smaller parts might integrate into each of these larger units? Compare answers with a partner.

1. an army
2. a public park
3. the European Union
4. a transportation network
5. an all-star soccer team
6. a neighborhood

C. Which of these things do you think should be rigid? Which are less rigid or can fluctuate depending on the situation? Write *R* for those that you think should be rigid and *F* for those that can fluctuate. Discuss your answers in a small group.

___ 1. bedtime for small children

___ 2. financial agreements between friends

___ 3. financial agreements between family members

___ 4. transport schedules (bus, train, plane)

___ 5. a teacher's grading system

___ 6. beliefs about what's good for the environment

___ 7. political views

Vocabulary Activities | STEP II: Sentence Level

Word Form Chart			
Noun	**Verb**	**Adjective**	**Adverb**
transformation	transform	transformative	_____

D. Answer these questions in your notebook. Use each form of *transform* at least once in your answers. Refer to Reading 1 for information. Compare sentences with a partner.

1. What is the most significant way Earth's landmasses have changed since the days of Pangaea?

2. As scientific thinking became more advanced in Europe, how did explanations of Earth's geology change?

3. How did continental drift affect Antarctica?

4. What role did the theory of plate tectonics play in the debate about continental movement?

5. What big change is likely in the arrangement of Earth's continents?

Word Form Chart

Noun	Verb	Adjective	Adverb
accommodation	accommodate	accommodating	accommodatingly
displacement	displace	displaced	_____
evolution	evolve	evolved evolving evolutionary	_____
restraint	restrain	restrained restraining	_____
reverse reversal	reverse	reverse	(in reverse)

E. Read another excerpt related to plate tectonics. Then restate the information in your notebook, using the word(s) in parentheses. Concentrate on main ideas and leave out the less important details. Be prepared to read aloud or discuss your sentences in class.

1. Continental drift is a powerful, ongoing process. Many geologists let their thoughts roam a few hundred million years in the future without letting Earth's present appearance distract them from what it will eventually look like. (*restrain*)

    *The minds of many geologists are not **restrained** by the Earth's present form.*

2. Using the principles of plate tectonics, they try to guess how the arrangement of the Earth's continents will change between now and 250 million years from now. (*evolve*)

3. Dr. Christopher R. Scotese, of the University of Texas at Arlington, predicts that the current continents will slowly join again, creating a new supercontinent, *Pangaea Ultima*. (*evolution*)

4. He and other geologists agree about other likely changes. As Africa moves north toward Europe, it will squeeze the Mediterranean Sea out of its location. A rugged range of "Mediterranean Mountains" will take its place. (*displace*)

5. An immense new landmass containing present-day Africa, Europe, and Asia—*Afrasia*—will form. Australia and Antarctica will run into it. Only a small basin will be left for a much smaller Indian Ocean. (*accommodate*)

6. South America will move north, pushing aside the islands of the Caribbean, until northern Venezuela crashes into southern Florida. The two Americas will together head west toward eastern Afrasia. (*displace*)

7. Scotese predicts that, about 200 million years from now, the westward-moving Americas will change direction and head east toward the other side of Afrasia. The Atlantic Ocean will disappear. (*reverse*)

8. Other geologists believe nothing will keep the Americas from moving west, as they are now. Dr. Sergei Pisarevsky of the University of Western Australia predicts that the Pacific Ocean will disappear. (*restraint*)

9. Many geologists agree that Pangaea Ultima will eventually form, and there are many different scenarios for how it might happen. When you're guessing about the next 250 million years, you have to be prepared for surprises. (*accommodation* or *accommodate*)

Before You Read

Read these questions. Discuss your answers in a small group.

1. Find the African countries of Eritrea, Ethiopia, and Djibouti on a map. What do you know about these countries or this area of the world?

2. On the map of Africa, what geological features indicate where a tear might be located on Earth's crust?

3. How do you think oceans form?

Read

This online news article examines a major geological event occurring in East Africa.

An Ocean Waiting to Happen

The nomads[1] were terrified. For a week in September of 2005, the ground shook violently. Cracks opened up in the soil, swallowing
5 goats and camels. Smoke rose out of the dark splits in the ground. After retreating to the hills, the nomads saw pieces of glassy rock burst **randomly**
10 through Earth's crust "like huge black birds" and fly almost 100 feet (30.5 meters) into the air. A cloud of ash dimmed the sun for three days. At night
15 the new crater[2] breathed flashes of fire.

Afar's desert with smoke or fire visible in the rift

"They had experienced earthquakes before but never anything like this," said Atalay Ayele, a scientist at Addis Ababa University, who
20 interviewed the Afar tribespeople in this isolated corner of northeastern Ethiopia. The Afar people did not know why the land was shaking and exploding.

Dr. Ayele and his colleagues knew the area
25 was geologically unstable, but the number of strong earthquakes was exceptional. There were 162 quakes measuring more than 4 on the Richter scale[3] in just two weeks—a quake measuring 5 on the scale releases as much
30 energy as the **nuclear** explosion that destroyed Hiroshima in World War II. All this

---

[1] *nomads:* members of a **community** that moves seasonally and has no permanent home
[2] *crater:* a large hole in the ground formed by natural processes
[3] *Richter scale:* the system for showing the strength of an earthquake

made Ayele's team suspect that something extraordinary had happened deep underground.

SPLITTING APART

When satellite data for the region became
35 available, they showed that huge forces had just **transformed** East Africa. Here in the Afar desert, one of the hottest and driest places on Earth, a new ocean was **evolving.** For the first time, observation of an event of this sort was possible,
40 **aided** by a satellite. Images from the European Space Agency's Envisat satellite showed that a huge rift, or crack, 40 miles (64 kilometers) long and up to 26 feet (8 meters) wide, had opened deep in Earth's crust. The tear was created by a
45 violent upsurge of molten rock. This magma pushed in along a break where two plates of Earth's crust meet. The magma **displaced** both plates, pushing them aside and apart.

Tim Wright, a geologist at the University of Leeds
50 who interpreted the satellite results, was astonished by the images and what they pointed to. "The process happening here is identical to that which created the Atlantic Ocean," he said. "If this continues we believe parts of Eritrea,
55 Ethiopia, and Djibouti will sink low enough to allow water to flow in from the Red Sea."

LAND OF DEATH

Teams from the United Kingdom, France, Italy, and the United States have gone on expeditions to Afar. This is the region described by the
60 explorer Wilfred Thesiger in the early 20th century as a "land of death." Satellites now give **comprehensive** views of what he meant. From above, you can see vast, **rigid,** black tongues of cooled lava reaching out into the
65 desert sands. Rust-colored volcanoes stand open and gaping, their lids blown off. There are so many fissures[4] and faults[5] where the ground has opened and slipped that Earth's "skin" looks like elephant skin.

70 The moon-like geography reflects what lies beneath. Afar stands at the junction of three tectonic plates, which meet at unstable fault lines. The Nubian and Somali plates run along the Great Rift Valley. The Arabian plate branches out

75 to the north. The boundaries of these plates continually **fluctuate** as the magma underneath pushes them around.

COLLISION AND DIVISION

Earth's tectonic plates are constantly shifting—usually by only a few centimeters a year.
80 Adjacent plates can slide past one another, as occurs along the San Andreas Fault in California. The plates can also collide. India's collision with the landmass to the north started its **integration** with the Eurasian continent. This
85 process forces the crust upward and creates mountain ranges, such as the Himalayas.

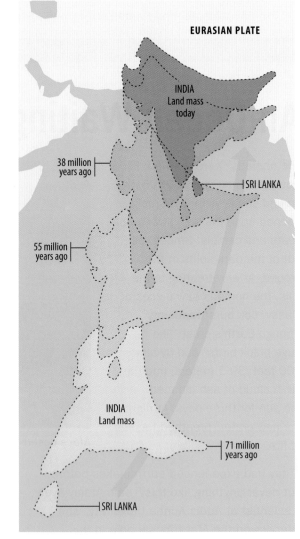

EURASIAN PLATE

INDIA
Land mass today

38 million years ago

55 million years ago

SRI LANKA

INDIA
Land mass

71 million years ago

SRI LANKA

Movement of the India land mass over the past 71 million years

Or the **reverse** could happen. Plates can also pull apart, causing continents to break up and

---

[4] *fissures:* small cracks, as in a rock or Earth's crust
[5] *faults:* large, deep cracks in Earth's crust

oceans to form. Early in this process, as the
90 distance between plates increases, the earth's
crust stretches and thins out. Magma rises up,
eventually cracking the thinned crust, and the
plates drift apart. Between the fault lines, the
crust, now heavy with cooled magma, sinks to form
95 a deep valley, often below sea level. The formation
of this depression is an **intermediate** stage in the
birth of an ocean. A bowl now sits ready to
accommodate water that rushes in from a nearby
sea as soon as there is an open channel.

100 This is how the Atlantic was formed, separating
Africa and Eurasia from the Americas. And this is
what scientists believe is happening in Afar as
the Arabian, Nubian, and Somali plates pull apart.

Parts of the region have already sunk to more
105 than 328 feet (100 meters) below sea level.
Only the highlands east and north of the
Danakil Depression **restrain** the Red Sea
from rushing in. Eventually, erosion or
quakes will create a break in the highlands,
110 and the depression will quickly become an
ocean floor. The new sea is predicted to be
formed within about a million years. The
complete separation of the Nubian and
Somali plates along the Great Rift Valley
115 could take ten times as long. At that time,
Africa will lose its distinctive horn as the
Somali Plate heads east.

Reading Comprehension

Mark each sentence as *T* (true) or *F* (false) according to the information in Reading 2.
Use the dictionary to help you understand new words.

___ 1. During the 2005 earthquakes, pieces of rock flew up randomly out of the ground.

___ 2. Water from the Red Sea has rushed into the Afar region.

___ 3. A rift is a kind of opening.

___ 4. Three tectonic plates come together in the Afar region.

___ 5. Before the 2005 earthquakes, the Afar region could accommodate farms.

___ 6. Despite the region's remoteness, the effects of the 2005 quakes have been extensively studied.

___ 7. Satellite photos of the Afar region show that a hole many miles long opened up in 2005.

___ 8. Scientists believe magma will rise up between the tectonic plates and displace them, pushing them farther apart.

___ 9. The Atlantic Ocean is the only thing restraining the new ocean from forming.

___10. Residents of Afar hope the new ocean will soon help relieve the extreme heat in the region.

APPLY

An author's choice of language can imply feelings or attitudes. Read these excerpts from Reading 2 and complete each implication that follows. Infer the adjective that best describes what the author means. Four of the adjectives will not be used. Check your dictionary for the meanings of new words. Compare answers with a partner.

accurate	incompetent	misleading	uninformed
avoidable	inevitable	perceptive	useful
difficult			

1. The Afar community did not know why the land was shaking and exploding.

   Implication: The Afar community was _____ .

2. All this made Ayele's team suspect that something extraordinary had happened deep underground.

   Implication: Ayele's team is _____ .

3. This is the region described by the explorer Wilfred Thesiger in the early 20th century as a "land of death." Satellites now give comprehensive views of what he meant.

   Implication: Thesiger's description was _____ .

4. Images from the European Space Agency's Envisat satellite showed that a huge rift, 40 miles (64 kilometers) long and up to 26 feet (8 meters) wide, had opened deep in Earth's crust.

   Implication: Envisat was _____ .

5. Eventually, erosion or quakes will create a break in the highlands, and the depression will quickly become an ocean floor.

   Implication: The formation of an ocean is _____ .

A. Complete the sentences about Africa's Rift Valley with the target vocabulary in the box. The synonyms in parentheses can help you. (Note: The sentences are not yet in order.)

accommodated	community	evolving	an intermediate
aided	displacement	fluctuated	restrain

___ a. "We are incredibly fortunate to have the Rift Valley," Leakey says, because that system has been _____ over the last 20 million years."
(forming)

___ b. During the course of its formation, the rift's new basins _____ water from rivers and seas, water that carried lots of sediment with it.
(made room for)

___ c. Leakey has had the good fortune to live in _____ period of the Rift Valley's history. The Eritrean and Ethiopian portions of the rift, in particular, are between an opening-up phase and a flooding phase.
(middle)

___ d. Leakey says the continuing _____ of land along the rift makes erosion possible in previously buried sediments, exposing new fossils.
(moving aside)

___ e. Maeve Leakey, of East Africa's most famous family of fossil-hunters, considers herself lucky to have worked in the Rift Valley. She cannot easily _____ herself as she describes the importance of the rift.
(control)

___ f. She also points out that "many of the rift sites, like Turkana, are badlands, which cannot be cultivated and are not threatened with buildings and concrete." Members of the scientific _____ are the only
(group with shared interests)
humans with a reason to spend much time there.

___ g. The Great Rift Valley runs from southern Lebanon to southern Africa's Zambezi Valley. Its dramatic geology has _____
(made things easier for)
anthropologists hunting for remains of distant human ancestors, especially in Eritrea, Ethiopia, Kenya, and Tanzania.

___ h. The sediments buried the bodies of dead of animals in the area, fossilizing bodies and animal bones. As water levels _____ with changes
(went up and down)
in the landscape, the process repeated itself several times.

B. Put the sentences in activity A into a logical account of Maeve Leakey's observations. (More than one order may be possible.) Read your sequence to a partner.

C. Read each of these pairs. What are some intermediate stages between the members of the pair? Write as many as you can in your notebook. Compare lists in a small group and discuss your ideas.

1. cold / hot

   cold...chilly...cool...mild...warm...hot

2. child / adult

3. college graduate / professor

4. office assistant / company president

5. blueprint for a house / a livable residence

6. running one mile a day / running a marathon

7. not knowing about something / becoming an expert at it

8. buying a camera / showing your movie to an audience

9. reading a recipe / serving dinner to family or friends

D. Read the sample sentences that feature forms of the word *accommodate*. Then answer the questions below in your notebook, using a dictionary as suggested. Compare answers with a partner.

> a. As our family grew, my parents had to keep building additions onto the house to **accommodate** us all.
> b. Making **accommodation** for Jim's disability was not hard, involving only a ramp at the front door and some new bathroom fixtures.
> c. The proposal is quite **accommodating** to the opposing party's demands.
> d. He **accommodated** the press a great deal, giving interviews and posing for pictures.

1. Check (✓) the word closest in meaning to *accommodate*. Consult your dictionary before you answer.

   ___ suit   ___ access   ___ compose   ___ embrace

2. Each of the sentences in the box above indicates that something was accommodated. What was it?

   a. _____

   b. _____

   c. _____

   d. _____

3. Look at the sample sentences in your dictionary for *accommodate* and its forms. What is being accommodated in each of those samples?

4. Does *accommodate* have any forms that are not used in the sample sentences in the box above? If so, what are they? Consult your dictionary.

Some of the changes the earth has undergone have been enormous. Some of them have been beneficial, some harmful, and some both, depending on which people you consider. For example, the Medieval Warm Period was certainly beneficial to the Vikings, who were able to explore farther than ever before. It was not so great, however, for the people the Vikings conquered during this period.

E. Each of these situations describes a big event or change on Earth. How might the change be beneficial? How might it be harmful? Who does (or did) it affect and how? Write a few sentences for each item in your notebook, using at least two of the target words in parentheses, in any form, in your answers. Be prepared to read aloud or discuss your ideas in class.

1. The ten hottest years, as measured by worldwide average temperatures, have occurred since 1998. There is no longer much serious doubt that the climate of the planet is getting warmer. (*fluctuate, reverse, random, transform*)

2. In 1991, a huge volcanic eruption at Mt. Pinatubo in the Philippines threw massive amounts of ash into the air. This hung in the atmosphere worldwide for most of the following 12 months and prevented sunlight from reaching Earth's surface. The planet's average temperature in 1991 was almost one degree Celsius lower than normal. Worldwide, 1991 was the third-wettest year on record and had the third-coolest summer. (*aid, community, nuclear, transform*)

3. From 1963 to 1967, a new volcanic island, named Surtsey, formed off the southwest coast of Iceland. (*accommodate, community, displace, evolve*)

4. In human history, Africa's climate has become significantly drier. The Sahara Desert has expanded many times over, making it almost impossible for people to live, grow crops, or raise animals there. (*aid, displace, restrain, reverse*)

5. In 1908, a gigantic explosion occurred over the forests of Siberia in Russia. About 80 million trees were instantly flattened. People more than 100 miles away were knocked down by the shock wave from the explosion. It was probably caused by an asteroid vaporizing as it streaked through Earth's atmosphere. (*nuclear, random, rigid, transform*)

6. Until about 7000 years ago, a land bridge existed across the Bering Strait. It connected northeast Asia and what is now Alaska. It formed because a series of ice ages locked a great deal of water into glaciers, lowering sea levels. (*accommodate, evolve, integrate, intermediate*)

F. Not everyone accepts the theories of continental drift and plate tectonics. Look at these arguments for and against it. Restate each idea in your notebook, using some form of the word in parentheses. Then write a paragraph that expresses your own opinion. Try to use as many target words as possible in your work. Be prepared to read your paragraph or debate this issue in class.

For	Against
There are many similarities among currently separate landmasses: similar fossils, similar mineral deposits, and similar geologic features. (*integrate*)	Landmasses are similar because they are all part of the same planet. There is no need to assume a supercontinent to explain these phenomena. (*random*)
Precise measurements have established that some pieces of Earth's crust are simply not in the same places they were 30 years ago. (*displace*)	Land moves all the time—sometimes slowly, sometimes quite fast—in such events as earthquakes and landslides. (*restrain*)
The theory of plate tectonics is scientific. It allows us to gather evidence, make predictions based on that evidence, and then test our predictions. It has done an excellent job of fitting in with observations experts have carefully recorded. (*accommodate*)	There are many traditional explanations of how the world took shape, and none of them mentions moving plates. Plate tectonics ignores wisdom that is thousands of years old. Scientists overestimate their abilities if they think truth has suddenly been discovered in the last 50 years. (*community*)

G. Self-Assessment Review: Go back to page 97 and reassess your knowledge of the target vocabulary. How has your understanding of the words changed? What words do you feel most comfortable with now?

Writing and Discussion Topics

Write about or discuss the following topics.

1. What geological phenomena or features are there in the area where you live? How might they have formed? How might they affect the climate of the region?

2. Look again at the events and changes in activity E on page 111. Choose one and do some research to find out more about it. Does your research change your mind about whether it was beneficial to anyone?

3. Plate tectonics may be useful in describing some other planets and some moons in our solar system. There is no evidence of present-day plate movement on any of these bodies, but it may have occurred in the past. On Mars in particular, more and more evidence suggests that there has been some movement of tectonic plates. What features would you expect to see on Mars if it once experienced the movement of tectonic plates? After you have made your guesses, go online and search for "mars tectonic." Were any of your guesses correct?

UNIT 8

Clicks and Cliques

In this unit, you will

> read about how young people form social groups in different school environments.

> review finding the main idea.

> increase your understanding of the target academic words for this unit.

READING SKILL Highlighting and Annotating

Self-Assessment

Think about how well you know each target word, and check (✓) the appropriate column. I have…

TARGET WORDS	never seen the word before	seen the word but am not sure what it means	seen the word and understand what it means	used the word, but am not sure if correctly	used the word confidently in *either* speaking *or* writing	used the word confidently in *both* speaking *and* writing
AWL						
arbitrary						
clause						
converse						
deviate						
diverse						
domain						
gender						
🔑 guarantee						
🔑 inevitable						
🔑 institute						
intervene						
maximize						
passive						
so-called						

🔑 Oxford 3000™ keywords

Before You Read

Read these questions. Discuss your answers in a small group.

1. Have you ever had to share a room or an apartment with someone? Did you already know the person? Describe the experience.

2. What possible conflicts might roommates have? Would these conflicts be less likely to occur if the people knew each other already? Why or why not?

3. Have you ever looked for information about a friend or acquaintance on the Internet? If so, why? Did you find anything? Do you think it's okay to look people up without telling them?

Read

This newspaper article is about an Internet tool for finding out about college roommates before you meet them.

Judging Roommates by Their Facebook Covers

Mailbox-watching is supposed to subside for North American high school seniors after they receive their acceptance letters and make their college choices. Each summer, however, many an
5 incoming freshman[1] anxiously waits for the mailbox to produce another crucial envelope— the one holding the name of his or her future roommate.

Many people assume that college freshmen pick
10 their dormitory roommates, as upperclassmen are allowed to do. The **converse** is actually true. Very few colleges allow incoming freshmen any choice in dorm-room assignments. It's **inevitable** that students will worry about potential problems
15 with a roommate—a complete stranger. Students in the **so-called** millennial generation, in particular, are anxious about sharing a room with another person. Many have never shared a room at home. They are used to their rooms
20 being their exclusive **domains**.

Roommates in their dorm room

ROOMMATE RESEARCH

For decades, residential-life offices have received late-summer telephone calls from worried students and parents. "People will read a name and address, and it fits into
25 some category in their head," says Sarah B. Westfall, dean of students at Denison University in Ohio. They expect a **diverse** student body at almost any college, but many students fear **diversity** as much as they look
30 forward to it. Any indication that a roommate's

---

[1] *freshman:* a first-year student at a four-year college, university, or high school

life **deviates** from the familiar can heighten a student's fear of the unknown. Online social-networking sites now allow students to get more of those indications than ever before.

35 According to college officials, many incoming freshmen use Facebook, Orkut, QQ, and other social-networking sites, to do research on their future roommates. Since everything happens anonymously[2], normally **passive** students can
40 spring into investigative action without having to approach a live person. On sites like these, anyone can post a profile of himself or herself free. Profiles can include photos, quotes, inside jokes, and lists of their favorite bands and TV
45 shows. The idea is to **maximize** your attractiveness to people with tastes similar to yours. Facebook has more than 750 million registered users, about 70% of whom are outside the United States. Orkut has about 66 million
50 users, mostly in Brazil and India. QQ, in China, is one of the largest social networks in the world, with more than 300 million active accounts.

PREVENTION BEATS INTERVENTION
Such profiles can help strangers break the ice before move-in day, but they can also cause alarm.
55 A student's fondness for a certain kind of music or room decorations can annoy a roommate before the two even meet. As a result, administrators are spending more time dealing with compatibility issues before students arrive. At some campuses,
60 residential-life counselors have decided it's easier to prevent roommate problems than to **intervene** in them later. Their offices have prepared guides to using profiles wisely. They mail these guides out right from the start, in the same envelope as the
65 notice of a roommate's identity.

Most students mistakenly believe the roommate-assignment system is **arbitrary**. The school[3] might separate students by **gender**, they think, but beyond that it's a matter of chance. Actually,
70 nearly every college prides itself on carefully considering each student's circumstances when assigning roommates. They don't **guarantee** roommates will get along, but they succeed much more often than they fail. They hate to see such
75 careful work undone by a single click of a

keyboard—especially since so many profiles are not exactly accurate.

NOT NECESSARILY TRUE
Clauses in the user agreements for social-networking sites set some rules for profiles,
80 but nothing in the agreement says they have to be true. Even students who use social-networking sites every day tend to forget that. For that reason, some schools have **instituted** "reality training" for social
85 networkers. "We try to explain to them that there is a lot of posturing that goes on," one advisor says. "Students are trying to create an image that makes them seem fun and cool, and they post things that may or may
90 not be true about themselves as a result." Admission officers also have students look at their own online profiles and ask, "What kind of roommate do I look like?"

Roommates with different personalities can still get along well.

BRANDI AND SARAH
Some students say it's natural to form instant
95 opinions when surveying their peers' profiles. Brandi, an incoming freshman at the University of Evansville in the U.S. state of Indiana, considers herself outgoing and easy to get along with. When she found out who
100 her roommate would be, Brandi went to a social-networking site, where she found Sarah's profile. Her excitement quickly turned to disappointment.

"Her page was all pink, and I thought, 'Oh,
105 gosh, we're not going to get along,'" says Brandi. "It said she was from California and into cheerleading, and I'm more into other

---

[2] *anonymously:* without giving one's name or identity
[3] *school:* In the United States, any educational **institution** at any level (including university) can be referred to as a school.

sports. She just seemed really girly." Brandi found hope in Sarah's profile, however. Both students had listed Tim McGraw and Faith Hill as two of their favorite country-music singers. Sarah had also posted many photographs of herself with friends, who looked like the sort of people in Brandi's own clique, or group of close friends. This convinced Brandi that her roommate was probably more similar to her than she thought.

So Brandi decided to give her future roommate a chance and sent her a message through the online network. This started a conversation. Two telephone calls later, her first impression had changed. Sarah has two younger siblings, ages 15 and 17, just as Brandi does. And now that Brandi knows that Sarah took a lot of Advanced Placement classes[4] in high school, she no longer pictures her roommate as a lazy or immature student.

"I think we're actually going to be really good friends," says Brandi.

---

[4] *Advanced Placement classes:* college-level courses taught in high school

Reading Comprehension

Mark each sentence as _T_ (true) or _F_ (false) according to the information in Reading 1. Use the dictionary to help you understand new words.

___ 1. Most universities arbitrarily match roommates in dorms.

___ 2. Students could get information about future roommates even before social-networking sites became available.

___ 3. Social-networking sites were instituted by colleges and universities.

___ 4. A social-networking profile can be designed to reflect one's tastes in music, favorite activities, and so on.

___ 5. Anyone placing a profile on a social-networking site must guarantee that the information is accurate.

___ 6. Brandi considers herself a quiet, passive person and was afraid her future roommate would be too outgoing.

___ 7. Music was the first common interest for Brandi and her roommate.

___ 8. Brandi decided not to contact her new roommate because social networking is not an accurate source of information.

READING SKILL

LEARN

After you read an article or chapter in a book, you may need to refer to the information again; for example, when you're studying for a test or writing an essay. Instead of copying the information you might need into a notebook, it is more efficient to *highlight* and *annotate* the reading.

Highlighting   Use a bright marker to make important passages easy to see. You might also want to underline or circle parts of the reading.

Annotating   Write little notes to yourself in the margins of the reading.

Highlight and annotate only the materials that you own! If you are borrowing a book, do not write in it.

APPLY

Follow the directions to highlight and annotate Reading 1. You will need a colored marker and a pen or pencil. Then, with a partner, use your annotations to answer the questions that follow as quickly as you can.

- First, highlight all the names of individual people.
- Second, circle each name of a college or university. In the margin next to each, write its location.
- Third, highlight or underline any statistics or important data in the article (look for numbers and source citations).
- Fourth, as you read, highlight any unfamiliar words you encounter. In the margin next to each, write a short definition using your dictionary.

1. What school is Brandi going to attend? _____

2. Where is Denison University? _____

3. How many registered users does Facebook have? _____

4. Where do most of Orkut's users live? _____

5. What other networking site is mentioned in the article? _____

6. What does *posturing* mean in this context? _____

7. Which musicians do Brandi and Sarah both like? _____

8. Who is the dean of students at Denison University? _____

REVIEW A SKILL Finding the Main Idea (See p. 20)

Look again at Reading 1. Find the main idea of each section of the reading. In sections 2, 3, and 4, the main idea is not the same as the heading.

1) Paragraph 2

2) "Roomate Research"

3) "Prevention Beats Intervention"

4) "Brandi and Sarah"

A. Read this advice about behaving properly on a social-networking website. For each item, cross out the one word or phrase in parentheses with a different meaning from the other three choices. Compare answers with a partner.

Every week or so, someone writes to me about a social networking problem. Maybe the writer is being bothered by someone, or maybe the writer posted something embarrassing. So here—just as a reminder—are six rules to keep in mind:

1. Writing a comment to everyone on your list might be nice, but why are you doing it? Just to (*raise / maximize / display / increase*) the number of comments on your page? That's lame. You know who you are.

2. The fact that someone takes time to read and comment on your blogs is a(n) (*sure sign / guarantee / assurance / source*) of affection. It proves the person cares about your inner thoughts. Don't ignore these comments.

3. Having 500 people on your list of (*nominal / so-called / supposed / dear*) friends and only 20 comments is a sign that you have to pretend people like you. Add only people you know to your list. Be as popular as you are—or aren't.

4. Never respond to a private message with a comment in the public (*arena / realm / domain / dialect*). That's rude.

5. If you post a personal 100-question survey, there's one (*questionable / unavoidable / inevitable / certain*) result: Nobody will read it.

B. What is the converse of each of these things? Is there more than one? Read your answers with a partner and discuss (or converse about) the different possibilities.

1. love: _____
2. youth: _____
3. happiness: _____
4. success: _____
5. passivity: _____
6. inevitability: _____

The word *intervene* means "to come between," usually to prevent or solve a problem. Although it is similar to *interfere,* intervening is usually seen as helpful and interfering is considered impolite and annoying.

Sometimes, the difference between *intervention* and *interference* depends on the perspective of the people involved. For example, a passenger in a car might give the driver directions because he thinks the driver is lost. The passenger sees this as intervention, but the driver might see it as interference and be insulted.

CORPUS

C. Check (✓) the situations in which you would intervene. Discuss your choices in a small group. Explain your perspective and decide whether the other people involved might consider your action (or inaction) interference.

___ 1. Two students in your class are discussing whether there is a test tomorrow. One says there is, the other says there's not. You know that there is.

___ 2. A confused-looking man you don't know is standing, with a map in his hand, on a street corner.

___ 3. Some of your friends are playing basketball. You can see that players from the other team are tripping and knocking down players on your friends' team.

___ 4. One of your friends is arguing with his or her father. You feel the father is being unfair.

___ 5. Two of your cousins, who have very different views, are arguing about which soccer team is the best.

___ 6. As you are walking to a special dinner in a nice restaurant, you see that a car is stuck in some mud. One person is trying to drive while another person pushes, but the car is not moving.

___ 7. You are watching your son's team play basketball, and the team is losing. You think you could give them some advice that would help them do better.

___ 8. Four or five students are standing around another student, insulting him and pushing him around.

Vocabulary Activities | STEP II: Sentence Level

Word Form Chart			
Noun	**Verb**	**Adjective**	**Adverb**
the converse	_____	converse	conversely
diversity	diversify	diverse	diversely
guarantee	guarantee	guaranteed	_____
inevitability	_____	inevitable	inevitably
passiveness	_____	passive	passively

D. Read another account related to college roommates. Then restate the sentences in your notebook, using the words in parentheses. Concentrate on main ideas and leave out details. Be prepared to read aloud or discuss your work in class.

1. Many college freshmen expect to socialize with their roommates, or even to be friends. They express surprise when things don't happen that way. (*converse*)

   Many freshmen expect to hang out and be friends with their roommate. They are often surprised when their real experience is converse to what they expected.

2. This probably happens because few freshmen really know what to expect. With no prior experience of anything like a roommate relationship, they may think of it as a sort of official friendship set up by the university. (*guaranteed*)

3. And it may start out that way. Two people lost on a large campus, with no acquaintances outside the dorm, will naturally look to each other for a social foundation. (*inevitably*)

4. Soon, however, each one's social network spreads wider through classes, clubs, parties, and chance meetings. (*diversify*)

5. If both roommates succeed equally at making such contacts, there is not likely to be a problem. But if one is significantly less active in making friends, some resentment may build up. (*passive*)

6. Straight talk about this situation in orientation sessions is very important. Shy freshmen who are prepared for it and see it as bound to happen are less likely to take it personally if it happens to them. (*inevitable*)

7. Those freshmen who are more socially successful can help a roommate who is experiencing things differently. (*the converse*)

8. Of course, no student has an obligation to make sure that his or her roommate has a good time. By college, young people are presumed to have developed some social skills of their own. (*guarantee*, verb)

Word Form Chart			
Noun	**Verb**	**Adjective**	**Adverb**
deviation deviant	deviate	deviant	_____

E. Write the answers to the questions in your notebook, using the form of *deviate* in parentheses. Refer to Reading 1 for information. Compare sentences with a partner.

1. Why are many college freshmen worried about rooming with a stranger? (*deviate*)

2. Is it abnormal behavior for someone to tell lies in a social network profile? (*deviant*, adjective)

3. Would it be typical for a college to allow freshmen to choose their own roommates? (*deviation*)

4. What do you think would happen if, after checking a social-networking site, a student thought a prospective roommate was dangerously abnormal? (*deviant,* noun)

5. Why did Brandi get upset after first seeing Sarah's profile? (*deviate*)

Before You Read

Read these questions. Discuss your answers in a small group.

1. Within the student body at your school (or at a school you used to attend), are there smaller social groups? Do they have names? What brings people together into these groups?

2. Do you belong to any social groups at your school (or at a school you used to attend)? Are these formal groups or just informal collections of friends?

3. Have you ever known anyone who seemed totally out of place at school, who had only a few friends or none at all? Describe that person. Why do you think that person was so out of place?

READING SKILL | Highlighting and Annotating

APPLY

After you read this article, you will answer these questions in a paragraph about 75 words long:

> *What social groups are there at Chaparral High School? What determines the social groups students are in?*

As you read, highlight and annotate the information you think will be valuable in your answer.

Read

This case study from a sociology textbook examines the social groups at a high school in the U.S. state of Arizona.

High School Society: Who Belongs Where?

At lunch time, look around the sprawling Chaparral High School campus in Scottsdale, Arizona, in the southwestern United
5 States. The social geography of the 1,850 students is clearly **instituted.** The football players and their friends have the center table outdoors. In back of them, other popular students
10 chat cheerfully—an attractive gathering of cheerleaders, lesser jocks[1], and members of the student government. If you qualify for membership under some unwritten
15 **clause** in the group's unwritten rulebook—even if no one has ever met you before—you've got it made. Lauren, a sophomore cheerleader, notes that "unqualified" students
20 would never dare sit where she's sitting. "But once you're in with the girls, everyone is really friendly to you. When I made cheerleader, it was like I was just set."

OTHER GROUPS
25 Inside, in the cafeteria, a **converse** society exists. There are more braces[2] and glasses and hair that doesn't quite have a shape. These are

the skateboarders, the **so-called** nerds[3], those who say they are just regular, the freshmen
30 who have not yet found their place. They may have lower social status than the sunny groups outside, but they generally feel they have, or eventually will have, a social place they can live with. There are many other lunchtime **domains**
35 as well. A group of art students eats in the studios, and some band members gather by the music building. Dozens of drama students eat in the theater building, where they are joined by some students whose looks or manners
40 **deviate** from the norm but who find the theater group more tolerant than most.

TAKING EVERYONE
Secondary schools worldwide are shaped by the natural tendency of teenagers to form exclusive social groups known as cliques. Despite all the
45 choices at Chapparal, a few students still have no clique. They eat upstairs or alone outside the library, or they just **passively** wander, their heads low as they pass groups of noisy

---

[1] *jocks:* athletes; people whose main interest is sports
[2] *braces:* teeth-straightening equipment applied directly onto the teeth
[3] *nerds:* people who are mainly interested in academics, especially math or science, and who are unconcerned about popular styles and activities

schoolmates. They are reminders that a U.S.
50 public high school has to admit all kinds of
students, but it cannot **guarantee** them all a
place in high-school society.

Chaparral is a large, well-regarded high
school in an affluent suburb. It is a pleasant
55 place, where parents, teachers, and students take
justifiable pride in their facilities, their
community, and their achievements. Compared
with big-city schools, these schools do not look
very **diverse.** The majority of the students are
60 white, middle class, and dressed in the same few
brand names. But the reality is far more complex.
Those who run such good suburban schools are
well aware that some of the most horrifying
school violence has happened at this kind of
65 place, not at tough inner-city high schools.

They speculate about the reasons for this.
The dropout rate in the U.S. has declined
sharply since the 1960s, especially in suburban
schools. Poor urban schools still lose many of
70 their problem students to the streets. Suburban
schools still have them. "It used to be that the
kids who were really having trouble, the
misfits, would leave," said John Kriekard, the
principal at Chaparral. But now, "we serve all
75 kinds of kids and we have to try to be all things
to all people."

He and others also emphasize the central
role schools play in suburban life. "In big cities,
there are lots of places where kids make
80 connections, where they have pieces of their
lives," he said. "But in a place like this, we're
pretty much it." This **maximizes** the influence
that school society has on a student's overall life.
Adolescence has always been a time of identity
85 formation, with inclusion and exclusion, trying
out new ideas, styles, and friends. And these are
not primarily girl issues. No matter what your
gender, good looks, cool friends, academic
achievement, and money have always defined
90 the social terrain.

TROUBLED TEENS

A few troubled students would continually
disrupt the whole school unless someone—if
not the principal, then the law—**intervened.**

These students are likely to be rootless and
95 poorly directed, and their chances of finding
effective control at home are slim. Economic
factors are less important than family factors
and previous social experience. Such behavior
is a call for help, not for material goods. To a
100 teenager who has little experience with
acceptance and security, these advantages seem
to be given **arbitrarily** to some people and not
to others, certainly not to them.

Some high school students feel alienated from their classmates.

Carol Miller Lieber, a former principal, says
105 many students entering high school already see
themselves as losers[4]. Not surprisingly, this
affects their perception of the entire school.
Studies show that students who see themselves
inevitably as outside the winners' circle have far
110 more negative views of a school than either the
teachers or the most successful students. "In
these big high-powered suburban high schools,
there's a very dominant winner culture,
including the jocks, the advanced-placement
115 kids, the student government and, depending on
the school, the drama kids or the service clubs,"
she said. "The winners are a smaller group than
we'd like to think, and high school life is very
different for those who experience it as the
120 losers. They become part of the invisible middle
and suffer in silence, alienated and without any
real connection to any adult." Interviews with
Chaparral students confirm the research: the
popular students who lunch outside were far
125 more likely than the ones sitting inside to say
that they love the school and feel connected to
at least one teacher. ■

---

[4] *losers:* (slang) persons who are not successful or not popular

Now, write the paragraph assigned to you in the Reading Skill on page 121. Use your highlighting and annotation to help you. Read your paragraph to a partner and discuss your ideas.

Reading Comprehension

Mark each sentence as *T* (true) or *F* (false) according to the information in Reading 2. Use the dictionary to help you understand new words.

___ 1. At Chaparral High School, athletes have the highest social position.

___ 2. Passive students must ask special permission from the school to eat lunch outdoors.

___ 3. Most students who don't fit in with any clique disrupt the whole school.

___ 4. Someone who becomes a cheerleader is guaranteed acceptance at that group's lunch table.

___ 5. Public schools in the U.S. are required to accept even troubled students.

___ 6. In a suburb, the school is likely to provide most of a student's social experience.

___ 7. The majority of students in a typical high school see themselves as winners.

___ 8. Social acceptance in high school leads to positive attitudes toward school.

Vocabulary Activities | STEP I: Word Level

A. Complete the sentences about social groups in high school using the target vocabulary in the box. Use each item one time. Use the synonyms in parentheses to help you. (Note: The sentences are not yet in order.)

clause	gender	inevitable	intervene
deviate	guaranteed	instituted	so-called
domain			

___ a. "When kids are tossed together every day, six hours a day, for the entire

school year," says psychologist Thomas J. Berdnt, "friendship groupings are

_____ ."
(impossible to avoid)

___ b. At one high school near Chicago, the social groups take their names

from the places students like to sit. The _____ "wall" people
(labeled)

are fashionable students who hang out at a bench along a wall near the

cafeteria. The "trophy-case" kids are students who sit on the floor under a

display of sports awards.

___ c. These "friendship groupings," better known as cliques, are small, tightly

knit groups that establish a social _____ for people who share
(territory)

interests or characteristics.

___ d. Cliques "can be based on appearance, athletic ability, academic

achievement, social or economic status, talent, seeming sophistication," or

ability to attract people of the opposite _____ , according to
(sex)

adolescent development experts Anita Gurian and Alice Pope.

___ e. Members of cliques often share the same values and exhibit the same

behavior. Although they have been known to form in elementary school,

cliques are more normally _____ among middle and high
(established)

school students.

___ f. Once inside a group, a student is careful not to _____ from
(go in a different direction)

any of the unwritten rules.

___ g. Someone with distinctive tastes in clothes, hairstyle, or music is almost

_____ to be considered part of a clique of people with similar
(certain)

tastes. This is true whether or not the student socializes with these people.

___ h. While every high school seems to have its own "jocks" or "nerds," the local

environment at a particular school may _____ and create a
(step into the situation)

special set of cliques.

B. Put the sentences in activity A into a logical order to describe high school social groups. (More than one order may be possible.) Read your sequence to a partner.

C. Many academic words are also considered formal words. Which of the target words in this unit (see the chart on page 113) are more formal synonyms for these informal words and phrases? Be sure to use the right forms of the target words.

Informal	Formal
1. by chance	_____
2. be different	_____
3. get involved	_____
4. opposite	_____
5. certain	_____

D. Read the sample sentences that feature forms of the word *diverse*. Then answer the questions below in your notebook, using a dictionary as suggested. Compare answers with a partner.

> a. **Diversity** of opinion makes our staff meetings very lively.
> b. My son's school is culturally **diverse**, so they celebrate 17 or 18 holidays every year.
> c. The company decided to **diversify** and make a wide range of products.
> d. A **diversified set** of investments will contain some stocks, some bonds, and some real estate.

1. Check (✓) the word closest in meaning to *diverse*. Consult your dictionary before you answer.

   ___ wayward

   ___ alien

   ___ variegated

   ___ complicit

2. Each of the sentences in the box above indicates that something is diverse. What is it?

   a. _____

   b. _____

   c. _____

   d. _____

3. Look at the sample sentences in your dictionary for *diverse* and its forms. What is diverse in each of those samples?

4. Does *diverse* have any forms that are not used in the sample sentences in the box above? If so, what are they? Consult your dictionary.

Vocabulary Activities | STEP II: Sentence Level

Most public high schools in the United States allow students a great deal of self-expression. Rules about clothing, hairstyles, jewelry, and other fashion items are quite loose. All this freedom can shock visitors from other countries—or even Americans who haven't seen a high school in 15 or 20 years.

E. In each of the situations below, a high school student engages in a kind of self-expression. For each situation, answer these three questions in your notebook:

    a. Is this contrary to normal behavior? How does it deviate from the norm?

    b. Should the school institute a rule against it? Why or why not?

    c. Should the right to do this be guaranteed? Why or why not?

Refer to the readings in this unit and your personal opinions.

1. A student wears a hat in class.

   It's unusual to wear a hat in class. I would call it rude. But it is not important enough to make rules about it.

2. Some students bring bottles of soda and drink them during class.

3. A girl wears white face makeup so thick and heavy it looks like a mask.

4. A student stands in front of his or her school and shouts criticism of the school's principal.

5. Two students text each other during class.

6. A student comes to school wearing dirty, wrinkled clothes.

F. Discuss your opinions about the situations in activity E in a small group. Then prepare an oral report that summarizes your discussion of one of the situations. Present your report to the class.

G. Look at these arguments for and against being part of a clique in high school. Restate each idea in your notebook, using some form of the word in parentheses. Then write a paragraph that expresses your own opinion. Try to use as many target words as possible in your work. Be prepared to read your paragraph or debate this issue in class.

For	Against
Students are able to better develop their special skills if they spend time with people who share their interests. For example, a student interested in literature needs to be around others who can discuss books and present opposing viewpoints. (*converse*)	By hanging out in groups of students much like themselves, students develop a narrow perspective. High school should be a time for exploring life's possibilities, not for restricting yourself. (*maximize*)
During the teen years, students need the security of a group of friends. They are moving away from the protected environment of home and need a safe, comfortable refuge. (*guarantee*)	Blending in too much with others discourages students from being individuals. Teenagers who could be leaders fail to step up, preferring not to call attention to themselves. (*passive*)
You cannot stop students from forming social groups. Rather than wasting time trying to tell students who they can socialize with, parents and the school should give these groups constructive things to do. (*inevitable*)	Teenagers appreciate the guidance of adults when it comes to choosing friends. When adults assert their experience, teens may act annoyed. In the long run, however, they will appreciate the help adults give. (*intervene*)

H. Self-Assessment Review: Go back to page 113 and reassess your knowledge of the target vocabulary. How has your understanding of the words changed? What words do you feel most comfortable with now?

Writing and Discussion Topics

Write about or discuss the following topics.

1. High school groups often form around common interests like music. What other interests unite students into a social group? What types of activities do these cliques enjoy?

2. As Reading 1 suggests, young people increasingly use the Internet to interact with other people. Describe some ways this is done. If you often communicate via the Internet, use some of your own experiences as examples.

3. Psychologists point out that, to a teenager, the opinions of friends are often more influential than the opinions of parents. Therefore, it is important for teenagers to choose their friends carefully. Do your friends influence you more strongly than your parents do? Why or why not? Are there things you can learn from friends that you cannot learn from parents? Explain.

UNIT 9

True and False

In this unit, you will

> read about factual accuracy in news stories and "reality" in news photographs.

> review previewing and predicting.

> increase your understanding of the target academic words for this unit.

READING SKILL Understanding Sequences

Self-Assessment

Think about how well you know each target word, and check (✓) the appropriate column. I have…

TARGET WORDS	never seen the word before	seen the word but am not sure what it means	seen the word and understand what it means	used the word, but am not sure if correctly	used the word confidently in *either* speaking *or* writing	used the word confidently in *both* speaking *and* writing
AWL						
amend						
apparent						
assign						
🔑 eliminate						
🔑 emphasis						
ethic						
🔑 grant						
ignorance						
insert						
levy						
perceive						
🔑 purchase						
🔑 restrict						
submit						
successor						

🔑 Oxford 3000™ keywords

Before You Read

Read these questions. Discuss your answers in a small group.

1. Have you ever known anyone who was the victim of a false rumor? Was the person harmed in any way? What happened?

2. How do news organizations gather information for their reports? What problems might they encounter when gathering it?

3. Do you think most of the news reports you receive are true? Why or why not? How can you know for sure whether they are true?

MORE WORDS YOU'LL NEED

account: a report or description of something that has happened
editor: a person who is in charge of a newspaper or part of a newspaper
journalism: the profession of collecting, writing, and publishing news
rumor: a piece of information or a story that people talk about, but that may not be true

---

REVIEW A SKILL **Previewing and Predicting** (See p. 2)

Review the "Previewing and Predicting" section in Unit 1. Look at the headings and photographs in Reading 1, "A Game of Checkers." What do you think the reading will be about?

 Read

This online news article discusses the dangers of inaccurate information in news reports.

A GAME OF CHECKERS

It was all a mistake, but that was no comfort to the Vorick family of southern California in the United States of America. On a cable television channel in 2005, a news commentator
5 said that the owner of a grocery store in the Los Angeles area was a terrorist and that he lived at a certain address in the town of La Habra. The address belonged to the Voricks. Day and night, people drove by their house
10 and shouted rude comments. Someone, **apparently** not the best speller in town, spray-painted "Terrist" on their property. The family's sense of privacy disappeared as strangers drove up, photographed the
15 house, and drove silently away.

News commentators need to verify facts before they present information.

The commentator should have checked his facts before he spoke. The man accused of being a "terrorist" had once lived at that

address, but that was before the Voricks bought
25 it. And another small thing: The man had never
been charged with terrorism or any other crime.
The cable network had a lot of apologizing to do.

WORTH THE EFFORT

Mistakes will happen, but the errors in this case
were easily preventable. Any college journalism
30 student would have known what to do: a simple
Internet search of property ownership in La Habra
and a quick check to see if the "terrorist" had
a police record. **Inserting** this one important
step in the process might have taken the staff
35 30 minutes or so. Carelessly skipping it was very
costly, both for the commentator (who lost his job)
and the cable network. Many advertisers are
nervous about **purchasing** air time on a network
that is **perceived** as careless. If either the Voricks
40 or the alleged[1] terrorist decides to file a lawsuit,
the court could **levy** huge penalties against the
cable network, the commentator, or both.

CHECKING EVERYTHING

Most magazines, television stations, and other
media outlets employ fact-checkers or
45 "researchers" of some type so they avoid trouble.
Fact-checkers are usually young, relatively
inexperienced members of the editorial staff.
When a report, script, article, or manuscript is
being prepared, the fact-checkers are **assigned** to
50 make sure everything is right. They check the
spelling of names, the accuracy of numbers, the
sequence of events, and the sources of
quotations. Their tools are Internet search engines,
dictionaries, history books, telephones, and public

Fact-checkers use several tools, including telephones
and the Internet, to do their job.

55 records of every sort. No questionable item
can be **ignored**. If they don't know whether
something is correct, they have to find out.

Most journalists believe they have an **ethical**
responsibility to be as accurate as possible.
60 Sometimes that involves fact-checking, but
sometimes it cannot. Daily newspapers do
not generally employ separate fact-checkers.
Reporters are expected to get the facts right
in the copy[2] they **submit**. A copy editor[3] might
65 occasionally question a "fact" that seems
incorrect, but newspapers operate under
severe time **restrictions**. Re-checking most
information is usually not possible.

For media that have deadlines that aren't as
70 short, the story is different. Some magazine
fact-checking departments are legendary for
their thoroughness. *The New Yorker* magazine
of the mid-20th century had a reputation for
fact-checking excellence. The magazine's
75 standards declined a bit in the 1970s and
1980s. Then, in the 1990s, managing editor
Tina Brown, **emphasizing** accuracy, hired the
people necessary to restore the department's
good reputation. According to one rumor,
80 there was an article that said a singer had
gestured with both arms. An eager fact-
checker called the singer and asked whether
he, in fact, had two arms. Even other
publications **granted** that *The New Yorker*
85 was the fact-checking champion. Jobs in the
fact-checking department at the magazine
became a desirable path to high-level
editorial jobs.

SERIOUS CONSEQUENCES

In far more cases, fact-checking departments
90 have been severely cut back or even
eliminated. When a checking staff is reduced,
the few checkers who remain cannot afford to
spend much time on any one issue. As a
result, some inaccurate stories have slipped
95 through the system. One account in
Newsweek in 2005, about the behavior of U.S.
soldiers, sparked religious riots that killed at
least 15 people. Because the story had never

---

[1] *alleged:* accused but not proven
[2] *copy:* written material intended to be printed in a newspaper
[3] *copy editor:* a person whose job is to correct and prepare text for printing

been fact-checked, *Newsweek's* editors could not
100 show evidence that it was true. It was based on
statements by only one source, and no one else
could verify⁴ it. Eventually the magazine
retracted⁵ the story, an indication that it was
probably not true. Of course, by that time the
105 damage had been done.

Good fact-checking early in a story's life is vital. Any errors must be **amended** right from the start. Once one magazine or television station has reported a story, others will 110 soon do the same. Consequently, mistakes get passed on and circulated widely. Even if they are eventually discovered, they are very hard to remove from what "everybody knows."

---

⁴ *verify:* confirm
⁵ *retracted:* said that something printed earlier should not have been printed

Reading Comprehension

Mark each sentence as *T* (true) or *F* (false) according to the information in Reading 1.
Use the dictionary to help you understand new words.

___ 1. A convicted terrorist once lived in the house that the Voricks purchased.

___ 2. The TV commentator who mentioned the Voricks' address lost his job.

___ 3. People distrust organizations that spread incorrect information.

___ 4. Most fact-checkers have a lot of experience in specialized fields.

___ 5. If a checker does not know whether a fact in a story is correct, he or she has an ethical duty to assign the story to another fact-checker.

___ 6. During the 1990s, *The New Yorker* had a very good fact-checking department.

___ 7. A clever fact-checker discovered that a singer mentioned in an article had lost an arm.

___ 8. *Newsweek* made a mistake by basing a story on statements that could not be checked.

___ 9. Some incorrect news stories have led to injury or death.

___10. An incorrect "fact" is likely to be repeated by other news outlets.

READING SKILL   Understanding Sequences

LEARN

Articles often contain sequences of events. Sequences are important to understand because they help the reader understand the order in which events occurred. Sequences are marked by several different types of signals:

- Time expressions: *in 2011, at the end of February, last week*
- Adverbs of sequence: *first, then, afterwards*
- Verb tenses: past, present perfect, past perfect

APPLY

Use the sequence signals in Reading 1 to complete the list of events related to each topic. Put the events in the proper time order.

The Voricks

a. *The alleged "terrorist" lives in the house the Voricks would buy.*

b. _____

c. _____

d. _____

The New Yorker

a. _____

b. _____

c. *Tina Brown becomes managing editor.*

d. _____

The *Newsweek* story

a. _____

b. _____

c. _____

d. _____

e. *Newsweek retracts the story.*

A. Read these excerpts from another article about a mistake on a television news show. For each item, cross out the one word or phrase in parentheses with a different meaning from the other three choices. Compare answers with a partner.

1. Imagine this: You go to a television station for a job interview. Someone walks into a room and (*seemingly / clearly / apparently / possibly*) calls your name. You follow.

2. The next thing you know, you're being interviewed on live television regarding an event you are totally (*expert / uninformed / ignorant / clueless*) about.

3. You start to see it might be a mistake, especially when you realize that the interviewer keeps addressing you by a name that is slightly different from yours. It's close, but not quite. The interviewer doesn't seem to (*notice / perceive / admit / see*) that anything is wrong.

4. You answer her questions (*hesitantly / reluctantly / unethically / unwillingly*) with general statements. Still, she keeps interviewing you.

5. This is what happened on a live news show aired by the British Broadcasting Corporation (BBC). Even the man who was supposed to be interviewed—but wasn't—(*admits / grants / concedes / hopes*) thought it was pretty funny.

6. The producer who called out for the guest in the waiting room should probably have (*emphasized / stressed / amended / highlighted*) the last name. The intended guest was a British commentator on Internet issues named "Guy." The man actually led into the studio was a computer expert, also named "Guy."

7. The wrong Guy probably (*submitted to / showed up for / put up with / tolerated*) the surprise question session because he thought it was some new kind of job interview.

8. The BBC apologized for the mistake, but they did not publicly (*assign / give / accept / attribute*) blame for it to anyone in their organization.

B. Match these expressions that use the word *grant* with their definitions. Compare answers with a partner.

___ 1. grant permission
___ 2. student grant
___ 3. grant admission
___ 4. grant an award
___ 5. take something for granted
___ 6. research grant
___ 7. "Granted, . . ."
___ 8. grant a wish

a. give a prize
b. give someone what he or she asks for
c. "Of course, . . ."
d. allow something to happen
e. money given to enable education
f. money given to enable scientific study
g. allow someone entry to a restricted area or organization
h. assume that something is true without confirming it

The word *perceive* has two meanings. It can mean "to become aware of something through the senses," usually through seeing or observation. It can also mean "to see or think of something in a particular way." Two people can see the same thing but perceive it quite differently. The noun form for both meanings is *perception*.

CORPUS

C. Check (✔) the things that humans can perceive. For each item that you check, explain to a partner different ways it might be perceived by different people.

___ 1. the crying of a baby

___ 2. a person's age

___ 3. the age of planet Earth

___ 4. someone else's emotions (fear, joy, etc.)

___ 5. a possible solution to a problem

___ 6. the colors of a rainbow

___ 7. electricity

___ 8. infection by a bacterium or virus

Vocabulary Activities | STEP II: Sentence Level

The words *ignore* and *be ignorant of* have the same root but very different meanings.

ignore   pay no attention to someone or something

be ignorant of   not know about something

The adjective *ignorant* can also describe someone who lacks knowledge or facts, and the noun *ignorance* refers to this meaning.

CORPUS

D. Rephrase these statements in your notebook, using the form of *ignore* that is right for the context. Compare sentences with a partner.

1. The driver was in a hurry and decided not to follow the speed limit.

   *The driver **ignored** the speed limit because he was in a hurry.*

2. The driver said he didn't know the speed limit had changed, but still got a ticket for speeding.

3. The police officer told him that not knowing the law is no excuse for breaking the law.

4. While the reporter was in Malawi she embarrassed herself several times because she wasn't familiar with the local customs.

5. The editor dropped the story because she felt the reporter had purposefully left out information that didn't support his point of view.

6. The editor told him that pretending not to notice a problem will not make it go away.

Word Form Chart

Noun	Verb	Adjective	Adverb
_____	_____	apparent	apparently
assignment	assign	assigned	_____
grant	grant	_____	for granted
submission	submit	submissive	submissively
successor succession	succeed	successive	successively

E. Read another account related to accuracy in journalism. Then restate the sentences in your notebook, using the words in parentheses. Change the form of a word if necessary to fit the grammar of your sentence. Concentrate on main ideas and leave out details. Be prepared to read aloud or discuss your work in class.

1. The *Washington Post*, from the capital city of Washington, D.C., is one of the most respected newspapers in the United States. In 1981, when drug use in the capital was a big national concern, a reporter for the *Washington Post* turned in a story, titled "Jimmy's World." It was about an 8-year-old drug addict. (*submit*)

2. The sad story created a stir, and the reporter, Janet Cooke, became a kind of media superstar. A few months later, she was given a Pulitzer Prize, the highest award in American journalism, for her work on the story. (*granted*)

3. Meanwhile, Washington's mayor, Marion Barry, launched a huge effort, involving dozens of city employees, to find Jimmy. (*assign*)

4. Despite their efforts, the city officials found no trace of Jimmy. It became clear that the boy did not exist. (*apparent*)

5. One investigation after another found problems not only with the story but also with Cooke's statements about her education and previous experience. (*successive*)

6. A few days after the prize was awarded, however, the *Post* gave in to pressure from skeptics. The paper confirmed that the story was a fake and issued an apology to its readers. (*submit*)

7. Cooke resigned from the *Post* and gave back her prize. She laid the blame for the problem on her editors, who, she claims, put unbearable pressure on her to produce a big story. (*assign*)

8. At the *Post*, publisher Dan Graham—who had inherited his powerful position from his legendary mother, Katherine Graham—set up measures to better check the credentials of reporters it plans to hire. (*successor*)

Before You Read

Read these questions. Discuss your answers in a small group.

1. There is a saying, "The camera doesn't lie." Do you think this is true? Why or why not?

2. Have you ever taken a picture that was not as good as you had hoped? What was wrong with it? Could you do anything to fix it?

3. You have probably seen pictures supposedly showing UFOs, the Loch Ness monster, the Yeti, or other controversial phenomena. Do you find the pictures convincing? Why or why not?

Read

This newspaper editorial examines the practice of using computer programs to "fix up" news photographs.

Playing with the Pixels

A freelance photographer working in Beirut, Lebanon, tried a little too hard to convey the horror of war. He altered at least two photographs he took there during
5 the summer of 2006. In one, he used computer software to darken and thicken smoke rising from bombed buildings. In another he **inserted** objects below and behind an F-16 fighter jet to make it look like the jet was firing multiple
10 missiles. In reality, the jet was firing no missiles at all, only a flare. He then **submitted** both pictures to a news service, which **purchased** them and sent them out for newspapers to use.

Unfortunately for the photographer, his
15 alterations were soon **apparent** to some sharp-eyed readers. Many Internet bloggers pointed out clues—buildings that appeared twice in the same picture, inconsistent shadows, identical vapor trails behind the "missiles." Within hours, the
20 news service stopped distributing the pictures and dismissed the photographer. Subsequently, they issued a statement that such fakery[1] was **unethical** and had no place in the news business.

Maybe so, but it happens regularly. Recently,
25 another U.S. news service got caught sending out an altered photo of an Alaskan pipeline worker. An Egyptian newspaper in 2010 altered a photo of Hosni Mubarak, then Egypt's president, during a visit to the United Nations in
30 New York. The fake photo showed Mubarak walking in front of other world leaders as if he were the most important. In the real, unaltered photo Mubarak is at the back of the group. In 2003, a California newspaper fired a photographer
35 for combining two pictures from Iraq, taken moments apart, into one. In 2004, the re-election campaign for U.S. President George W. Bush reluctantly admitted altering a video by **inserting** faces into a crowd of soldiers listening to Bush.

An original image (left) and an altered version of it (right)

---

[1] *fakery:* falseness

40 You could tell because some faces appeared at several places in the crowd at the same time. Some of these episodes were relatively trivial[2] but others were quite serious attempts to mislead the public. All of them undermine the
45 public's trust in the reality of news photographs.

A camera with a long lens can show details no human eye can see.

Actually, that's good. The public tends to **assign** too much "reality" to what they see in photographs anyway. We should approach all news photos as somewhat unreal.

50 What does it mean for a photograph to be true? That it captures what we would **perceive** if we were standing where the camera was? That's nonsense. A camera sees quite differently from a human eye. "Normal" human vision is roughly
55 equivalent to what you get from a 35 millimeter camera lens zoomed out a little bit—to between 42 mm and 50 mm. A lens longer than that shows details no human eye could see. A lens shorter than that shows an unnaturally broad
60 view and too little detail.

There are **restrictions** to the way any camera can capture an image. Details that you or I could easily see in person may be lost in glare or sunk in a dark spot. Is it okay, then, to
65 use photo-editing software to **emphasize** such details and **amend** the "inaccurate" picture? Doing this would, in some ways, make the photo more accurate. What about **emphasizing** lost details that would *not* be visible to an
70 eyewitness? That would make the photo more accurate in other ways. Should news organizations **grant** their photographers permission to do that? If not, then should we ban photos taken through microscopes? You can
75 see how quickly the situation gets confused.

---

2 *trivial:* of little importance

Of course, photographers "alter" every photograph they take, simply because they have to make choices about how to take it. They have to decide where to stand, how to stand, whether
80 to put a filter on the lens, and so on. Editors alter them as well, literally and figuratively. Long before digital photography came along, newspaper editors chopped the edges off photographs, enlarged them, and **eliminated**
85 scratches or spots with correction fluid. Photo-editing software is simply a far smarter **successor** to those tools. Editors also write headlines and captions, words that can dramatically affect the viewer's **perception** of
90 the image. A picture of a fallen tree is just a fallen tree—until words tell you whether it's a good thing (Land Cleared for New Hospital) or a bad thing (Storm Downs 200-Year-Old Oak Tree). What you see when you contemplate a
95 news photo is what you're told to see.

Sometimes **perception** is controlled by what you're allowed to see. When U.S. President Ronald Reagan visited Germany's Bitburg cemetery in 1985, his aides **levied** strict
100 limitations on photographers. They could shoot only from certain vantage points. From these sites, they could not get both the president and the graves of Nazi soldiers in the same shot. The pictures that came out of that event certainly
105 weren't fake, but were they really true? Another U.S. president, Franklin Delano Roosevelt, (in office 1933–1945), had a disease called polio, and used a wheelchair every day throughout his presidency. Yet no major American newspaper or
110 magazine published a picture of him in a wheelchair through that entire 12-year period. The editors of these publications were not **ignorant** of the president's disability. The White House did not keep photographers away. The
115 editors simply didn't want the public to get the impression that their president was too weak to govern. Looked at as a whole, was the photographic record of FDR's presidency true?

Needless to say, news photographers
120 shouldn't doctor photographs any more than reporters should make up quotes. But "doctoring" is a slippery concept, and photographic truth is an illusion. ∎

Reading Comprehension

Mark each sentence as *T* (true) or *F* (false) according to the information in Reading 2. Use the dictionary to help you understand new words.

___ 1. The photographer in Lebanon apparently did not add anything by altering his photos.

___ 2. The news service submitted a public apology for sending out the altered photos from Lebanon.

___ 3. A presidential campaign once released a video altered to eliminate some people who were at an event.

___ 4. Sometimes, altering a photo has no truly serious consequences.

___ 5. A photographer alters a photograph simply by deciding how to take it.

___ 6. The best definition of a "true" photograph is that it shows what someone on the scene would see with his or her eyes.

___ 7. Photo-editing software can emphasize light or shadow.

___ 8. Photos taken through a microscope are not actually photos at all.

___ 9. Franklin Roosevelt was photographed with his wheelchair, but leading newspapers were reluctant to publish the pictures.

___10. It is a mistake to believe that photographs tell the truth.

READING SKILL | Understanding Sequences

APPLY

A. What sequence is described in paragraphs 1 and 2 of Reading 2? List at least six events in that sequence, in order.

Event

_____

_____

_____

_____

_____

_____

B. Write a short paragraph in which you put the events from paragraph 8 of Reading 2 into chronological order. Use at least five events and include signals.

_____

_____

_____

_____

_____

_____

_____

_____

_____

A. Complete the sentences about nature photography by using the target vocabulary in the box. Use each item one time. Use the synonyms in parentheses to help you. (Note: The sentences are not yet in the correct order.)

amend	emphasize	inserted	restrict
an apparently	ignores	perceived	successor
eliminated			

___ a. Ansel Adams, a master of American landscape photography, blacked out inconvenient elements from his photographs. Artistic considerations demanded that he _____ (stress) some things and play down others.

___ b. Eliot Porter was a pioneer in using color in nature shots. He hated dishonest photos but showed no reluctance to _____ (alter) nature as necessary. He once cut a cactus to pieces to get a shot of a roadrunner's nest.

___ c. In 1982, *National Geographic* put a digitally altered photo of Egypt's Pyramids of Giza on one of its covers. Ever since, there have been calls to _____ (limit) the use of computers to alter photos.

___ d. No one wants to be _____ (viewed) as favoring fake photos. In 1991, the National Press Photographers Association (NPPA) came out against digital manipulation by saying, "We believe it is wrong to alter the content of a photograph in any way that deceives the public."

___ e. Manipulation with photo-editing software is simply the _____ (follow-up) to earlier darkroom techniques used by history's best photographers.

___ f. It is _____ (a seemingly) reasonable policy, but it _____ (does not pay attention to) some practices that are common among photographers.

___ g. The great Paul Strand was also very much opposed to doctoring photos, but even he drew in manhole covers or _____ (took out) people from photos to make shots look better.

___ h. A photo promoting an Australian TV program showed three famous chefs plus a digitally _____ (added) image of a famous figure with spaghetti on his head. The photo was considered disrespectful and led to widespread protests.

B. Put the sentences in activity A into a logical sequence. (More than one order may be possible.) Read your sequence to a partner.

C. Many academic words are also considered formal words. Which of the target words in this unit (see the chart on page 129) are more formal synonyms for these informal words and phrases? Be sure to use the right forms of the target words.

Informal	Formal
1. buy	_____
2. to get rid of	_____
3. give	_____
4. notice	_____
5. hand in	_____
6. change	_____

D. Read the sample sentences that feature forms of the word *submit*. Then answer the questions below using a dictionary as suggested. Compare answers with a partner.

> a. **Submit** your application and a copy of your resume to the Human Resources Department.
> b. None of my **submissions** to the magazine has ever been accepted.
> c. A wolf will indicate **submission** to the pack leader by putting its ears back and tucking its tail between its legs.
> d. Even the president has to **submit** to the law.

1. The word *submit* has two main meanings. Check (✓) the word most similar to each meaning. Consult your dictionary before you answer.

    Meaning 1: ___ apply ___ withdraw ___ satisfy ___ offer

    Meaning 2: ___ defer ___ resist ___ supply ___ suffer

2. Which sample sentences in the box above go with each meaning?

    Meaning 1: _____

    Meaning 2: _____

3. Look at the sample sentences in your dictionary for *submit* and its forms.

    For meaning 1, what is being submitted?

    _____

    For meaning 2, what is being submitted to?

    _____

4. Does *submit* have any forms that are not used in the sample sentences in the box above? If so, what are they? Consult your dictionary.

    _____

    _____

    _____

Editors make changes to most news stories their reporters submit. Some of these are small changes like punctuation, grammar, or spelling. Others affect the content of a story. These changes could be made for several reasons:

- Some information in the original is inaccurate.
- The editor is worried that something in the story will cause the paper to be sued or will offend people.
- The editor or owner doesn't like a story's thesis or point of view.

Editors might also assign a story and tell a reporter what point of view to take.

E. Each of these situations involves a decision, by an editor or some other manager, that some people perceive as unethical. For each situation, answer these questions:

a. What apparent reasons were there for the action?

b. How did the emphasis of the story change?

c. Was the decision justified? Why or why not?

Refer to the readings in this unit and your personal opinions.

1. A reporter submitted a negative review of a restaurant that advertised frequently in his newspaper. The editor rejected it. He had a positive review written and published it instead.

_____

_____

_____

2. The sheriff's office asked the town's newspaper to insert a false story about a house fire, and the paper agreed. The fake story was used to catch a suspect who had offered to pay someone to set the fire. The story was the "proof" that the fire happened. The suspect paid the person, which confirmed the suspect's guilt.

_____

_____

_____

3. A high government official changed parts of a scientific research report on global warming. The original report emphasized that Earth's climate is definitely heating up. The official eliminated that language. His new version said that the "apparent" warming is not necessarily related to climate change.

_____

_____

_____

_____

F. Discuss your opinions about the situations in activity E in a small group. Then prepare an oral report that summarizes your discussion of one of the situations. Present your report to the class.

G. Look at these arguments for and against the digital alteration of news photographs. Restate each idea in your notebook, using some form of the word(s) in parentheses. Then write a paragraph that expresses your own opinion. Try to use as many target words as possible in your work. Be prepared to read your paragraph or debate this issue in class.

For	Against
If a photographer sees that a photograph fails to communicate what was actually happening, he or she has an obligation to fix it. Cameras can distort reality. (*emphasis / eliminate*)	A photograph should speak for itself. Viewers who see the photograph differently from the photographer may be able to sense things the photographer missed. (*perceive*)
Unlike earlier methods of repairing negatives, digital alterations do not ruin the original photo. People concerned about accuracy can compare altered and unaltered versions. (*restrict*)	Although several versions of a digital photo can coexist, the only one that matters is the one that is published. The first shot placed before the public creates a lasting impression. (*submit*)
No one wants to forbid the use of flashes or special lenses, but people feel free to tell a photographer how to use a computer. (*reluctance*)	Photo software can do things never imagined for other methods of photo manipulation, like adding and deleting things in the image. (*insert / eliminate*)

H. Self-Assessment Review: Go back to page 129 and reassess your knowledge of the target vocabulary. How has your understanding of the words changed? What words do you feel most comfortable with now?

Writing and Discussion Topics

Write about or discuss the following topics.

1. Fashion magazines in many countries have sometimes digitally edited photos of clothing models to make them look more beautiful. This is meant to make designer clothes look better on them. In your opinion, is this a good practice? Explain your point of view.

2. The essayist Susan Sontag once wrote, "The photographer is not simply the person who records the past, but the one who invents it." What do you think this statement means? Do you agree with it?

3. In many countries, newspapers and magazines include a section where they apologize for mistakes they have made in earlier issues. Such a retraction might say something like, "We apologize for incorrectly reporting Mr. Lee's occupation as 'duck driver.' He is a truck driver." If a newspaper printed incorrect information about you, would such an apology be enough to make you feel better? Should the newspaper do anything else to make up for the error? Would you be willing to sue the newspaper in court?

UNIT 10

Bites and Stings

In this unit, you will

> read about the consequences of being bitten or stung by certain insects or spiders.
> review outlining.
> increase your understanding of the target academic words for this unit.

READING SKILL Recording Processes with Flow Charts

Self-Assessment

Think about how well you know each target word, and check (✓) the appropriate column. I have...

TARGET WORDS	never seen the word before	seen the word but am not sure what it means	seen the word and understand what it means	used the word, but am not sure if correctly	used the word confidently in *either* speaking *or* writing	used the word confidently in *both* speaking *and* writing
AWL						
append						
🔑 chemical						
🔑 circumstance						
🔑 contact						
🔑 estimate						
external						
initiate						
minimal						
neutral						
🔑 percent						
regime						
🔑 sufficient						
🔑 summary						
virtual						

🔑 Oxford 3000™ keywords

Outside the Reading What do you know about dangerous insects? Watch the video on the student website to find out more.

Before You Read

Read these questions. Discuss your answers in a small group.

1. What kinds of ants are you familiar with? Where do they live? How do they come into contact with humans?

2. Have you ever been stung by an ant, bee, or wasp? How did it feel? What did you do to reduce the pain? How long did the effects last?

3. Name some animals that produce a poison to help protect them against enemies. How strong is their venom? Is it harmful to humans? How does the animal get its venom into the enemy's body?

MORE WORDS YOU'LL NEED

diagnosis: a doctor's opinion about what illness a person has

therapy: treatment to help cure an illness or injury

tissue: bodily material; there is bone tissue, muscle tissue, nerve tissue, etc.

venom: poison produced in an animal's body for self-defense or to kill prey

Read

This excerpt is from a book on insects in everyday life. It discusses a type of insect that is a growing threat in the United States.

Attack of the Fire Ants

The red fire ant, *Solenopsis invicta,* is one of over eighty thousand species of ants worldwide. Like their close relatives, 5 the bees, many species of ant have a sharp **appendage**, called a stinger, at the end of their body. Most bees can sting only once, and then they die. An ant's stinger can be used repeatedly.

A red fire ant

10   The red fire ant is not native to North America. It arrived on ships from South America in the 1930s through the port of Mobile, Alabama. That landing in Alabama **initiated** a full-scale invasion. Since then, fire ants from this 15 invasion have spread throughout the southern United States and Puerto Rico. The ants have also made their way to Australia, New Zealand, and China.

ANT ZONES

Following World War II, **circumstances** in the 20 U.S. worked in the ants' favor. The fire ant is known as a "tramp" or "weed" species because it thrives (like a weed) in recently cleared or disturbed areas. After the war there was rapid population growth in the "Sunbelt" of America's 25 south and southwest. Land cleared for new homes, parks, and factories was a perfect habitat for fire ants. Now, similar conditions in rapidly developing areas of Asia may prove inviting to the ants.

30　　By 1950, the ants in the U.S. had made it halfway up the border between Mississippi and Alabama. Since then, they have become firmly established in Texas, and they are relatively common in Arizona. A few have shown up in
35 California. They may eventually move into some milder parts of Oregon and Washington.

Public health experts **estimate** that, in any given year, from 30 to 60 **percent** of people living in *Solenopsis* zones in the United States
40 are stung. The ant grasps the skin with its tiny, powerful jaws, arches its body, injects the stinger into the skin, and releases venom. If not stopped, the ant will rotate itself around and create a whole circle of stings. There's an
45 immediate burning sensation, followed by hours to days of intense itching. **Virtually** everyone who is stung by a fire ant develops a red welt that stays painful for several days. Up to half of the victims will experience larger reactions near
50 the location of the bite.

SERIOUS REACTIONS

Fire ant venom may be toxic to the nervous system. One tree cutter in Florida suffered serious fire ant attacks three times within one year. After the third attack, his right hand and
55 forearm became numb[1] and his wrist became weak. This condition lasted for about a month. The venom is also *necrotic*—it kills the tissue that it comes in **contact** with. If this necrosis, or tissue death, happens after a
60 sting, permanent scars may remain on a victim's skin. Terrible sores can result if an infection takes hold near the necrotic tissue. The most
65 dangerous physical response to a *Solenopsis* sting, however, is an anaphylactic reaction. This is the same kind of reaction some people have to bee stings and is
70 similar to an extreme allergy. It begins with weakness, itching, chest tightness, and wheezing[2]. This can bring on a sharp fall

in blood pressure and sometimes even death.
75 In some fire-ant zones, fire ant venom causes more fatal reactions than bee stings. In sensitive people, a single sting is usually enough to **initiate** the reaction.

Fire ant venom is a watery solution of toxin
80 that affects human mast cells. These cells are filled with a **chemical** called "histamine." Histamine is the same **chemical** that triggers the sneezing, itching, and other symptoms of an allergy. When an allergy-causing substance
85 enters the body, the walls of the mast cells weaken until they can no longer contain the histamine. The cell explodes, releasing a rush of histamine. If these histamine explosions occur in the lungs, the reaction can be serious—
90 perhaps including a blockage of the passages that deliver air to the lungs. These lung problems are not common, but they are a real threat to anyone extremely sensitive to fire-ant venom.

Nothing can completely **neutralize** the
95 effects of fire-ant venom, but people sensitive to it who live in fire-ant territory have some treatment choices. Immunotherapy is currently the best option for **minimizing** reactions. It consists of a series of injections, administered
100 on a regular schedule. At first, patients receive very small amounts of fire-ant venom that their bodies can tolerate. With each injection, the amount of venom is increased, which causes the person's body to start building up
105 resistance to it. Eventually, patients have **sufficient** defenses to tolerate a fire-ant sting.

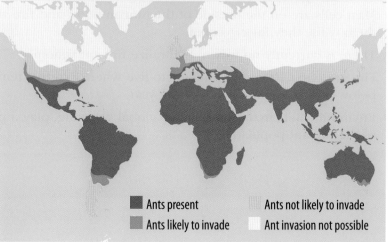

WORLD DISTRIBUTION OF FIRE ANTS

■ Ants present　　　　　■ Ants not likely to invade
■ Ants likely to invade　　□ Ant invasion not possible

---

[1] *numb:* not able to feel anything
[2] *wheezing:* difficult, noisy breathing

The immunotherapy **regime** is expensive, and it also requires a long-term commitment. Doctors **estimate** that treatments will take as

110 long as two years.

TEMPERATURE BOUNDARIES

Fire ant populations have not yet established themselves very far north. Many, many studies have tried to discover which temperatures are too cold for them. In **summary**, research shows

115 that, like any insect, a fire ant becomes less active as the weather grows colder. Eventually, it becomes totally motionless. Fire ants hit this temperature boundary at about 50° Fahrenheit (10° Celsius). Above that temperature, ants are

120 active. Below it, the ants slow down and can barely move.

In places where temperatures stay at least this low for much of the year, ant colonies cannot survive outdoors. In the U.S., at least for

125 the moment, this keeps the fire ants from attacking areas east of the Pacific Coast mountain ranges and north of the Ohio River. Worldwide, *Solenopsis* ranges as far south as the southern tips of South America, Africa, and

130 Australia. In the Northern Hemisphere, it does not generally spread north of 30 degrees north latitude and cannot survive north of 45 degrees north latitude. These statements, however, are based on climate conditions in the early 21st

135 century. What if the climate changes? Some health officials worry that global warming may open the door for the ant armies to march farther north.

A more immediate worry is that ant

140 colonies may take hold inside heated buildings. Under these **circumstances, external** temperatures would make no difference at all, and fire ants would become a much bigger problem for humans. ■

Reading Comprehension

Mark each sentence as *T* (true) or *F* (false) according to the information in Reading 1. Use the dictionary to help you understand new words.

___ 1. Red fire ants, like bees, deliver painful bites with their jaws.

___ 2. *Solenopsis invicta* first entered the United States through Puerto Rico.

___ 3. As the population in the U.S. South grew after World War II, more habitats for *Solenopsis* opened up.

___ 4. Very few people living in fire-ant territory ever come into contact with *Solenopsis*.

___ 5. Most people stung by red fire ants do not realize it until several hours later.

___ 6. *Solenopsis* venom can damage nerves and kill cells it touches.

___ 7. Mast cells are on the outside of the human body, and fire ants hold onto them while they inject venom.

___ 8. There is currently no way to neutralize fire-ant venom.

___ 9. Fire ant populations are unlikely to live where external temperatures go below 50° Fahrenheit much of the year.

___10. Environmental circumstances, like global warming, play a part in the spread of the fire-ant population.

LEARN

A process described in a reading may be simple and direct, or it could be quite complex. Sometimes, the direction of a process can depend on circumstances. It will take one direction if A happens and another direction if B happens.

A good way to clarify these possibilities in your notes is to use a flow chart. A flow chart shows how one event leads, or flows, into another. It also shows how circumstances might alter the process.

APPLY

A. Fill in this flow chart that traces the spread of fire ants in the U.S. Refer to Reading 1 for information. Note: The dotted line indicates a future possibility.

B. Fill in this flow chart showing what can happen as a result of a fire-ant sting. See Reading 1 for information.

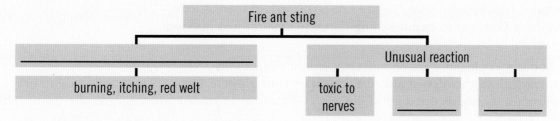

C. In your notebook, create your own flow chart to describe what happens in each "unusual reaction" to a fire-ant sting. See Reading 1 for information. Compare and discuss your flow charts with a partner. Your charts may not be exactly the same.

REVIEW A SKILL Outlining (See p. 52)

In Unit 5, you outlined a reading passage. An outline is an alternative to a flow chart. complete the following outline of the main sections in Reading 1.

I.   Introduction (Paragraph 1)

II. _____ (Paragraphs 2 and 3)

III. What happens when a fire ant bites (Paragraphs 4 and 5)

IV. _____ (Paragraphs 6 and 7)

V.   Geographical range of fire ants (Paragraphs 9 and 10)

A. Read these excerpts from an article on an organic gardening website. The author is giving advice on how to get rid of fire ants without using chemicals. For each excerpt, cross out the one word or phrase in parentheses with a different meaning from the other three choices. Compare answers with a partner.

1. There are several ways to kill a colony of fire ants without using poisonous (*chemicals / substances / appendages / compounds*) that could harm you or the environment.

2. An effective method that requires (*minimal / no / very little / minor*) effort is to "bucket" the colony. After shoveling a mound of ants into a large bucket, simply drown them by mixing soapy water into the sand in the bucket.

3. You could also pour hot water onto the ant mound. Because the water is chemically (*safe / neutral / harmless / virtual*), it does not damage the soil.

4. Unfortunately, a single treatment with hot water is usually not (*desirable / sufficient / satisfactory / enough*) to kill all the ants in a colony. You'll probably have to repeat the application at least three times.

5. Introducing some (*outside / external / local / exotic*) predator, such as straw mites, can kill ants. Unfortunately, then you have to find a way to get rid of *them*.

6. You probably could kill a colony by pumping exhaust fumes from your car into the mound. I (*estimate / argue / figure / guess*) it would take at least 45 minutes of running your car to begin killing them, instead of just making them unconscious.

7. Remember that household cleaners are chemicals. (*Almost / Especially / Virtually / Practically*) all of them pose a threat to you or your garden. Pouring them on an ant mound is not a good idea.

The word *contact* comes from a Latin word meaning "touch." In today's English, the verb *contact* usually means "to reach someone for the purpose of communicating."

*They were finally able to **contact** their daughter four days after the storm.*

For less important or shorter-term connections, people often use the phrase *come into contact with* or *come in contact with*.

*She works in a language school, so she **comes into contact with** people from all over the world.*

CORPUS

B. Check (✓) the people or things you have come into contact with. Then discuss your experiences with a partner.

___ 1. the headmaster or principal of your school

___ 2. a dangerous animal

___ 3. a celebrity

___ 4. people from another part of the world

___ 5. a gangster or dangerous person

___ 6. something mysterious or hard to explain

___ 7. serious illness

___ 8. an extremely rich person

Vocabulary Activities STEP II: Sentence Level

Word Form Chart			
Noun	**Verb**	**Adjective**	**Adverb**
estimate estimation	estimate overestimate underestimate	estimated overestimated underestimated	_____

C. Answer these questions in your notebook, using the word in parentheses in your answer. Refer to Reading 1 for information. Compare sentences with a partner.

1. About how long does an immunotherapy regime last? (*estimate,* noun)

   A typical **estimate** *is that it can last two years.*

2. About how many species of ant are there? (*estimate*, verb)

3. About what percentage of the population will get stung in ant territory, according to experts? (*estimated*, adjective)

4. If someone told you that he planned to complete an immunotherapy regime in a month or two, what would you say to him? (*underestimate*)

5. What would you say to a state official who wanted to require everyone in fire-ant territory to get immunotherapy? (*overestimate*)

6. In your opinion, should someone who is sensitive to ant stings live in Arizona? (*estimation*)

Word Form Chart

Noun	Verb	Adjective	Adverb
circumstance	_____	circumstantial	circumstantially
initiation initiative initiator	initiate	_____	_____
minimalization	minimalize	minimal	minimally
neutralization	neutralize	neutral	_____
sufficiency insufficiency	suffice	sufficient insufficient	sufficiently insufficiently

D. Read another account related to insect bites and stings. Then restate the information in your notebook, using the word in parentheses. Concentrate on main ideas and leave out the less important details. Be prepared to read aloud or discuss your sentences in class.

1. Staying away from venomous insects will not entirely protect us. (*sufficient* or *insufficient*).

   Avoiding venomous insects is **insufficient**.

2. The bites of non-venomous insects can produce many more serious illnesses than the bites of venomous ones. (*initiate*)

3. For one thing, venomous insects account for only a tiny percentage of the insect species on the planet. (*minimal*)

4. Also, the bacteria and other microorganisms carried by insects can do much more damage to a human body than most venoms can. The insect bite itself is not damaging enough to cause a problem. (*sufficiently* or *insufficiently*)

5. For some diseases, like malaria or Lyme disease, the insect is not the dangerous organism but just a carrier. Such carrier insects—including flies, ticks, and mosquitoes—are called "vectors." (*neutral*)

6. Mosquitoes are the most dangerous vectors. About 40 percent of the world's people live in conditions that expose them almost constantly to mosquitoes, including the type that carries malaria. (*circumstance*)

7. Most insect venoms and their effects can be counteracted by simple medicines. This is not the case with diseases carried by vectors. (*neutralize*)

8. Governments and nonprofit groups have launched several earnest efforts to reduce the effects of malaria, especially in tropical Africa, Southeast Asia, and Central America. (*initiative*)

9. Although these programs are important and somewhat effective, it is doubtful whether anything humans do could make a big difference in the threat that malaria poses. (*sufficient* or *insufficient*)

Before You Read

Read these questions. Discuss your answers in a small group.

1. Think about an incident in which you got insect or spider bites. Where were you when you were bitten? How did you react?

2. In your home town or home region, which insects are a problem? Do they bite? What happens to someone bitten by them?

3. Have you ever been bitten by an insect or spider you did not see? Why didn't you see it?

🔊 Read

This article from a popular online health magazine focuses on the importance of proper diagnosis and treatment of bites.

You Wouldn't Know It If It Bit You

The young woman had been looking forward to her nice new apartment in Manhattan. **Circumstances** turned out to be less comfortable than she expected, as this posting
5 to an online forum about insect bites shows:

> I just moved into a newly renovated
> apartment and got 10 huge, itchy bug
> bites on my arms, legs, and hip. I thought
> it was my mattress, so I got rid of it and
> 10 bought a new one. Still got bites and
> could not find bugs anywhere. I even tried
> freezing out my apartment by leaving the
> door open during the winter chill since
> I heard the bugs can't survive in temps
> 15 less than 25 degrees. No luck. I went to
> a dermatologist who said the bite pattern
> isn't like any of the usual apartment pests,
> and he didn't know what it was. I am
> miserable. My immune system has reacted
> 20 to the bites, and I have prickly itching ALL
> over my body, not just where the bites are,
> all day long. I called my landlord who is
> sending an exterminator over. Will post
> to let you know how it goes. If anyone
> 25 has found the solution, please email me.
> Thank you!

Bedbugs, shown at 4× actual size

UNSEEN BITERS

Every night, countless people crawl into bed knowing exactly how the writer feels. Instead of a peaceful night's sleep, they will get a new
30 round of bites by some mysterious pest. Because they don't know what's plaguing them, they have no idea how to stop it. In extreme cases, a concern becomes an obsession. Weakened by a lack of sleep, a
35 victim develops a feeling that biting creatures are everywhere. Bites and the fear of them establish a cruel **regime,** ruling the victim's daytime thoughts and nighttime dreams.

Bites by arachnids—such as spiders and
40 ticks— and by insects such as horseflies,

mosquitoes, or bedbugs are extremely common. **Virtually** all humans who survive past infancy are bitten at some point in their lives. A bite, which involves a creature's mouth parts, is different from a

45 sting, which is made with a sharp structure **appended** to a creature's rear end. Most insect bites cause only **minimal** discomfort, if any at all. The bite might cause a little swelling because **chemicals** in the bug's saliva[1] irritate the skin. More serious

50 problems are rare. When they do happen, the bite victim's own behavior might be to blame. Your parents **summarized** it for you when you were young: "Don't scratch those bites!" Scratching can open the skin and allow bacterial infections to get started.

55 Insects and arachnids account for almost all the bites people suffer, but they are identified less easily than any others. If a dog, a rodent, a horse, or even a snake bites you, you know that it has happened and which creature did it. If an insect

60 or spider bites you, you may not even feel the **contact** of its mouth parts with your skin. You may realize you've been bitten only after an itchy bump develops a few hours later. Even if you did feel a bite, you probably could not identify the

65 biter. Bugs are small. They move quickly. They have evolved excellent methods of staying hidden. Only a small minority of biting pests are even seen, much less swatted or captured. More often, the victims are left to wonder what bit them.

Brown recluse spider

LOOK-ALIKE MARKS

70 The body's reaction to a bite may not help narrow down the suspects. Different biters can cause the same symptoms. For example, many Australians who develop puffy red spots on an arm or leg blame white-tail spiders, mostly because white-

75 tails are extremely common. However, the sore

spot may be caused by the bite of an insect or another spider, or even by **contact** with a fungus. Another confusing situation involves two arachnids common in the eastern United

80 States—the deer tick, which can spread a serious sickness called Lyme disease, and the brown recluse spider, whose venom is strong enough to make human victims quite sick. Deer tick and brown recluse bites leave similar

85 **external** marks on a victim: a rash that looks like a bull's-eye target, with alternating rings of dark and light skin.

Guessing a biter's identity is no game. Being wrong can be dangerous. Doctors in Australia

90 have developed effective medicines, known as antivenins, to treat bites from some of the continent's many venomous spiders. Each antivenin, though, is specific to the venom from one type of spider. No other antivenin is

95 **sufficient** to **neutralize** the poison. There are risks as well when a North American doctor decides whether a bull's-eye bite mark comes from a deer tick or a brown recluse. If it's a tick bite but is treated as a spider bite, the

100 victim will not get antibiotics to fight Lyme disease, which causes serious heart or nerve conditions in about 10 **percent** of infected people. If it's a brown recluse bite but is treated as a tick bite, the spider's venom will

105 do greater damage. One serious effect of long exposure to strong spider venoms is necrosis, or "tissue death." Full-strength venom kills the skin, nerve, and muscle cells it touches, and the more **contact,** the more necrosis.

110 That's why it's vital to correctly identify any biting spider and **initiate** treatment with the proper antivenin as soon as possible.

The frustrated victim of unknown bugs in her Manhattan apartment did not suffer from either

115 Lyme disease or necrosis. Few people do. That does not mean she had things easy. We can easily understand her confusion—and her discomfort—as itching overtakes us after a day at the beach (sand fleas? spiders?), an hour on

120 the bus (mites? flies?), or a few minutes of strolling through a grassy field (nearly anything).

---

[1] *saliva:* the liquid that is produced in the mouth

Reading Comprehension

Mark each sentence as *T* (true) or *F* (false) according to the information in Reading 2. Use the dictionary to help you understand new words.

___ 1. The bugs that bit the Manhattan woman lived in her mattress.

___ 2. The fear of being bitten can create emotional problems.

___ 3. Scratching a bite can create health problems.

___ 4. Insects and spiders are the only animals likely to bite humans.

___ 5. Insects and spiders often go away long before a bite victim even discovers the bite.

___ 6. The consequences of failure to identify the source of a bite are mostly emotional, not medical.

___ 7. Most of the spider bites in Australia are caused by white-tailed spiders.

___ 8. Lyme disease is spread to humans through contact with mosquitoes.

___ 9. The venom of a spider can be neutralized by a medicine called an "antivenin."

___10. Necrosis can be prevented by a simple course of antibiotics.

READING SKILL | Recording Processes with Flow Charts

APPLY

Use the information in Reading 2 as a starting point for a flow chart. In your notebook, describe one of these things:

- what happens following a bite by a bedbug
- what happens following the bite of a venomous spider

To expand your chart, do some outside research on the process you choose.

A. Many academic words are also considered formal words. Which of the target words in this unit (see the chart on page 145) are more formal synonyms for these informal words? Be sure to use the right forms of the target words.

Informal	Formal
1. attach	_____
2. enough	_____
3. guess	_____
4. outside	_____
5. start	_____

B. Complete the sentences about Bee Sting Therapy (BST) using the target vocabulary in the box. Use each item one time. Use the synonyms in parentheses to help you. (Note: The sentences are not yet in the correct order.)

chemicals	initiates	neutral	regime
circumstantial	minimal	percentage	sufficient
in contact with			

____ a. Apitherapy uses _____ produced by bees—including venom—
   (substances)
   to promote human health.

____ b. BST's advocates say it is _____ to reduce the effects of a
   (powerful enough)
   serious inflammatory disease called multiple sclerosis (MS).

____ c. Scientists struggle to remain _____ on the subject of
   (not taking any position)
   apitherapy. On the surface, it just seems like a weird idea.

____ d. It seems to have gained popularity through _____ evidence,
   (situational)
   such as that only a small _____ of beekeepers develop cancer.
   (proportion)
   That is not enough for most health professionals.

____ e. Many eventually have only _____ control of some muscles.
   (very little)
   They may also experience problems with vision, internal organ function, or

   brain function.

_____ f. Perhaps the most controversial form of apitherapy is Bee Sting

Therapy (BST). The name says it all. Patients deliberately place bees

_____ their skin and wait for the sting.
            (against)

_____ g. Proponents of BST claim that a steady _____ of treatments
                                                        (regular system)

provides relief for sufferers of arthritis and other conditions involving

inflammation. Exactly how it does so has not been explained.

_____ h. The inflammation in MS typically _____ a slow deterioration
                                                    (starts)

of the central nervous system as it damages nerve cells.

C. Put the sentences in activity B into a logical order to describe BST. (More than one order may be possible.) Read your sequence to a partner.

The word *circumstance* comes from Latin words meaning "around" and "stand." In English, *circumstance* does not mean "standing around," but there is a connection to this idea. Circumstances are the general conditions surrounding a person, thing, event, etc.

CORPUS

D. Read the sample sentences that feature forms of the word *circumstance*. Then answer the questions below in your notebook, using a dictionary as suggested. Compare answers with a partner.

a. The ice storm was an unfortunate **circumstance,** wrecking our plans to have a nice dinner out.
b. Under other **circumstances** I would say "yes," but I have too much work to do.
c. His presence at the store on the night of the robbery is just **circumstantial** evidence.
d. Bob disappeared under suspicious **circumstances.**

1. Check (✓) the word closest in meaning to *circumstances*. Consult your dictionary before you answer.

___ periods   ___ intricacies   ___ commotions   ___ conditions

2. In each of these sentences, the circumstances "stand around" something. What is it?

3. Look at the sample sentences in your dictionary for *circumstance* and its forms. In those sentences, what do the circumstances "stand around"?

4. Does *circumstance* have any forms that are not used in the sample sentences in the box above? If so, what are they? Consult your dictionary.

Pesticides are chemicals used to kill insects or other small organisms that cause problems for people. Some pesticides are relatively harmless to humans. Others have been shown to cause great harm.

E. In each of the situations below, a pesticide is used. For each situation, answer these questions:

　　a. What chemical is it?

　　b. How is it being used?

　　c. Do the benefits of the pesticide outweigh its risks? Why or why not?

　　d. Under what circumstances should it and should it not be used?

　　Refer to the readings in this unit and your personal opinions.

1. Collars for pets often contain pesticides meant to kill fleas and ticks. Some collars contain a class of chemicals called *organophosphates*. In some studies, these chemicals show a connection to brain cancer, paralysis, and nerve damage in humans.

　　_____

　　_____

　　_____

2. DDT is a pesticide that kills mosquitoes and other insects. In the past, DDT was blamed for almost wiping out many species of birds, killing helpful bees on farms, and causing premature births. Its supporters say its ability to kill mosquitoes helps reduce the spread of diseases like malaria. Malaria kills about 1 million people each year and makes about 300 million sick. No human is known to have died from exposure to DDT.

　　_____

　　_____

　　_____

3. In 2011, about 600 cases of West Nile Virus were reported in the United States. Of these, more than 30 resulted in death—a death rate of about 5 percent. DDT is the most effective and affordable pesticide available to kill the mosquitoes that carry it.

　　_____

　　_____

　　_____

F. Discuss your opinions about the situations in activity E in a small group. Then prepare an oral report that summarizes your discussion of one of the situations. Present your report to the class.

G. Look at these arguments for and against a worldwide ban on the use of DDT. Restate each idea in your notebook, using some form of the word in parentheses. Then write a paragraph that expresses your own opinion. Try to use as many target words as possible in your work. Be prepared to read your paragraph or debate this issue in class.

For	Against
DDT does not poison just the places where it is used. By getting into the water supply, into fish populations, and other cross-border resources, it threatens the entire world. (*chemical*)	Before the U.S. banned DDT in the 1960s, it was sprayed over entire farms. Of course it spread through the environment. Now, DDT is used mostly as a spray for the walls of homes in mosquito-infested areas. (*minimal*)
Big chemical companies are no longer able to sell DDT in rich countries. They are eager to sell it instead to poor countries, regardless of the damage it might cause. Only a worldwide ban can protect relatively powerless citizens from this toxin. (*sufficient*)	Rich countries are able to keep developing nations poor and powerless by making sure malaria rates stay high. A ban on DDT would remove almost the only affordable tool these countries have for becoming healthier and more productive. (*circumstances*)
Widespread use of DDT has led to the emergence of resistant mosquitoes. In a sense, its use has made it ineffective. By stopping the spread of DDT use—and restricting it to true emergencies—we can protect the usefulness of this pesticide. (*neutral*)	DDT does not have to kill mosquitoes to provide protection from malaria. It is also a powerful repellant, effective even with mosquitoes resistant to it. It greatly reduces the chances that a human will be bitten by a mosquito indoors. (*contact*)

H. Self-Assessment Review: Go back to page 145 and reassess your knowledge of the target vocabulary. How has your understanding of the words changed? What words do you feel most comfortable with now?

Writing and Discussion Topics

Malaria and Lyme disease are not the only vector-borne diseases causing problems for humans. There are thousands of others, perhaps hundreds of thousands. No one knows for sure. Nor does anyone know how many people suffer from vector-borne diseases. According to figures from the World Health Organization, at least 600 million people (most of them in the tropics) have serious vector-borne diseases. Those with less serious ones almost certainly bring the total to more than one billion.

Write about or discuss the following topics.

1. a. Do a little research to find out more about one of these vector-borne diseases. How is it caused? Which parts of the world are hit worst by it? What kind of creature carries it? What are its effects on human health?

   • yellow fever

   • leishmaniasis

   • trypanosomiasis

   • dengue fever

   b. Why are the tropics especially hard hit by vector-borne diseases?

2. Success at fighting or avoiding vector-borne diseases has made possible a lot of human achievements. For example, the Panama Canal could not have been built if yellow fever had not first been brought under control. Agriculture and livestock ranching have expanded into areas where people once could not live and work because of the vector-borne diseases. How were these victories over disease accomplished? Were those methods good or bad for the overall environment?

3. Reading 1 says that global warming might affect the spread of red fire ants. What other effects might climate change have on biting or stinging insects and arachnids? Why? How would the changes you mentioned affect human health?

The Academic Word List

Words targeted in Level 2 are bold

Word	Sublist	Location	Word	Sublist	Location	Word	Sublist	Location
abandon	8	L1, U7	attain	9	L1, U5	complex	2	L4, U2; L0, U1
abstract	6	L3, U5	attitude	4	L4, U6	component	3	L4, U3
academy	5	L3, U1	attribute	4	L3, U10	compound	5	L4, U6
access	4	L1, U2	**author**	6	**L2, U4**	**comprehensive**	7	**L2, U7**
accommodate	9	**L2, U7**	authority	1	L1, U6	comprise	7	L4, U9
accompany	8	L1, U2	automate	8	L3, U6; L0, U7	compute	2	L4, U8
accumulate	8	**L2, U4**	available	1	L3, U5; L0, U6	conceive	10	L4, U10
accurate	6	L4, U6; L0, U2	aware	5	L1, U5	concentrate	4	L3, U8
achieve	2	L4, U1; L0, U9				concept	1	L3, U1; L0, U10
acknowledge	6	L1, U7	behalf	9	L3, U9	conclude	2	L1, U6
acquire	2	L1, U4	benefit	1	L4, U2; L0, U9	concurrent	9	L4, U5
adapt	7	L4, U7	bias	8	L4, U8	conduct	2	L1, U9
adequate	4	**L2, U4**	bond	6	L4, U3	confer	4	L4, U4
adjacent	10	**L2, U3**	brief	6	L3, U6	confine	9	L1, U10
adjust	5	L4, U3	bulk	9	L4, U9	confirm	7	L4, U10
administrate	2	L1, U3				conflict	5	L1, U2
adult	7	L3, U6	capable	6	L1, U8	conform	8	L4, U7
advocate	7	L1, U10	capacity	5	L4, U9	consent	3	L4, U7
affect	2	**L2, U6; L0, U10**	category	2	L4, U5	**consequent**	2	**L2, U3; L0, U4**
aggregate	6	L1, U9	cease	9	L4, U10	considerable	3	L3, U8
aid	7	**L2, U7**	challenge	5	L3, U8	consist	1	L4, U2, U9; L0, U7
albeit	10	L1, U7	channel	7	L1, U3	constant	3	L4, U8
allocate	6	**L2, U6**	chapter	2	L3, U7	constitute	1	L1, U4
alter	5	L1, U1	chart	8	L3, U10	constrain	3	L1, U8
alternative	3	L1, U10	**chemical**	7	**L2, U10**	construct	2	L3, U1; L0, U5
ambiguous	8	L1, U4	**circumstance**	3	**L2, U10; L0, U8**	consult	5	L1, U6
amend	5	**L2, U9**	cite	6	L4, U10	**consume**	2	**L2, U2; L0, U10**
analogy	9	L1, U4	civil	4	L1, U4	**contact**	5	**L2, U10**
analyze	1	**L2, U3; L0, U01**	clarify	8	L4, U8	contemporary	8	L1, U7
annual	4	L1, U9	classic	7	L3, U9	context	1	L1, U4
anticipate	9	**L2, U3**	**clause**	5	**L2, U8**	contract	1	L3, U9
apparent	4	**L2, U9**	code	4	L4, U9	**contradict**	8	**L2, U2**
append	8	**L2, U10**	**coherent**	9	**L2, U5**	contrary	7	L1, U6
appreciate	8	L3, U5	coincide	9	L1, U5	contrast	4	L1, U7
approach	1	L3, U1; L0, U10	collapse	10	L4, U10	contribute	3	L1, U9
appropriate	2	L1, U8	colleague	10	L1, U5	**controversy**	9	**L2, U3**
approximate	4	L3, U4	commence	9	L3, U9	convene	3	L1, U4
arbitrary	8	**L2, U8**	comment	3	L3, U3	**converse**	9	**L2, U8**
area	1	L4, U1; L0, U5	commission	2	L3, U9	**convert**	7	**L2, U2**
aspect	2	L3, U4	**commit**	4	**L2, U6; L0, U8**	convince	10	L1, U3
assemble	10	L3, U10	commodity	8	L4, U6	cooperate	6	L1, U2
assess	1	L1, U8	communicate	4	L3, U2	**coordinate**	3	**L2, U6**
assign	6	**L2, U9**	**community**	2	**L2, U7; L0, U4**	**core**	3	**L2, U5**
assist	2	**L2, U5; L0, U4**	compatible	9	L1, U9	**corporate**	3	**L2, U2**
assume	1	**L2, U1; L0, U4**	compensate	3	L3, U4	correspond	3	L3, U9
assure	9	L3, U4	**compile**	10	**L2, U6**	couple	7	L3, U1
attach	6	L3, U7	complement	8	L1, U7	**create**	1	**L2, U1; L0, U1**

Oxford 3000™ words

Word	Sublist	Location
credit	2	L3, U6
criteria	3	L3, U3
crucial	8	L3, U10
culture	2	L4, U10; L0, U6
currency	8	L3, U9
cycle	4	L4, U5
data	**1**	**L2, U3; L0, U10**
debate	**4**	**L2, U4**
decade	7	L1, U7
decline	5	L1, U2
deduce	3	L4, U7
define	1	L3, U2; L0, U4
definite	7	L3, U4
demonstrate	3	L1, U5
denote	8	L4, U6
deny	7	L4, U10
depress	**10**	**L2, U4**
derive	1	L4, U10; L0, U10
design	2	L1, U1; L0, U5
despite	4	L3, U2
detect	8	L1, U6
deviate	**8**	**L2, U8**
device	**9**	**L2, U3**
devote	9	L3, U9
differentiate	7	L1, U4
dimension	4	L4, U5
diminish	9	L4, U4
discrete	**5**	**L2, U6**
discriminate	6	L1, U10
displace	**8**	**L2, U7**
display	6	L3, U5; L0, U8
dispose	7	L4, U6
distinct	2	L3, U7
distort	9	L3, U6
distribute	1	L4, U8
diverse	**6**	**L2, U8**
document	3	L4, U9
domain	**6**	**L2, U8**
domestic	4	L1, U3
dominate	3	L1, U5
draft	5	L3, U6
drama	8	L3, U5
duration	9	L4, U1
dynamic	7	L1, U5
economy	1	L1, U7
edit	6	L4, U8
element	2	L4, U1
eliminate	**7**	**L2, U9**
emerge	**4**	**L2, U1**

Word	Sublist	Location
emphasis	**3**	**L2, U9**
empirical	7	L3, U4
enable	5	L3, U10
encounter	10	L3, U5
energy	**5**	**L2, U5**
enforce	5	L4, U7
enhance	6	L3, U1
enormous	10	L3, U8
ensure	**3**	**L2, U5; L0, U6**
entity	5	L4, U5
environment	**1**	**L2, U1; L3, U8; L0, U3**
equate	**2**	**L2, U2**
equip	**7**	**L2, U3**
equivalent	5	L3, U10
erode	9	L1, U9
error	4	L1, U10
establish	1	L1, U6
estate	6	L4, U6
estimate	**1**	**L2, U10**
ethic	**9**	**L2, U9**
ethnic	**4**	**L2, U1**
evaluate	2	L1, U10
eventual	8	L4, U3
evident	1	L4, U2; L0, U8
evolve	**5**	**L2, U7**
exceed	6	L4, U1
exclude	3	L4, U7
exhibit	**8**	**L2, U5**
expand	5	L1, U7
expert	6	L3, U8
explicit	6	L1, U3
exploit	8	L1, U5
export	1	L1, U3
expose	5	L3, U5
external	**5**	**L2, U10**
extract	7	L3, U2
facilitate	5	L4, U1
factor	1	L3, U8; L0, U4
feature	2	L4, U1; L0, U2
federal	**6**	**L2, U3**
fee	6	L1, U1
file	7	L4, U6
final	2	L4, U3
finance	**1**	**L2, U2**
finite	7	L1, U9
flexible	6	L3, U9
fluctuate	**8**	**L2, U7**
focus	2	L3, U8
format	9	L4, U8

Word	Sublist	Location
formula	1	L4, U8
forthcoming	10	L4, U3
found	9	L4, U8
foundation	7	L4, U4
framework	3	L1, U1
function	1	L3, U1; L0, U1
fund	3	L3, U3
fundamental	5	L4, U4
furthermore	6	L4, U9
gender	**6**	**L2, U8**
generate	5	L1, U5
generation	5	L1, U7
globe	7	L3, U2
goal	4	L3, U3
grade	7	L1, U7
grant	**4**	**L2, U9**
guarantee	**7**	**L2, U8**
guideline	8	L3, U3
hence	4	L3, U5
hierarchy	7	L3, U4
highlight	8	L4, U3
hypothesis	4	L4, U7
identical	7	L4, U5
identify	1	L4, U2; L0, U7
ideology	7	L4, U6
ignorance	**6**	**L2, U9**
illustrate	3	L4, U9
image	5	L3, U5
immigrate	**3**	**L2, U1**
impact	2	L1, U9
implement	4	L1, U2
implicate	4	L4, U7
implicit	8	L1, U3
imply	3	L4, U7
impose	4	L1, U10
incentive	6	L1, U10
incidence	6	L3, U10
incline	10	L1, U7
income	1	L1, U3
incorporate	6	L4, U4
index	6	L1, U4
indicate	**1**	**L2, U4; L0, U10**
individual	1	L1, U1
induce	8	L3, U7
inevitable	**8**	**L2, U8**
infer	7	L1, U8
infrastructure	8	L4, U6
inherent	9	L1, U1

Oxford 3000™ words

Word	Sublist	Location
inhibit	6	L1, U5
initial	3	L3, U7; L0, U8
initiate	**6**	**L2, U10**
injure	2	L1, U1
innovate	7	L1, U3
input	6	L3, U6
insert	**7**	**L2, U9**
insight	9	L3, U7
inspect	8	L3, U3
instance	3	L1, U6
institute	**2**	**L2, U8**
instruct	6	L4, U2
integral	9	L1, U4
integrate	**4**	**L2, U7**
integrity	10	L3, U7
intelligence	6	L3, U8
intense	8	L1, U2
interact	3	L1, U8
intermediate	**9**	**L2, U7**
internal	4	L3, U7
interpret	1	L3, U3
interval	**6**	**L2, U5**
intervene	**7**	**L2, U8**
intrinsic	10	L4, U4
invest	**2**	**L2, U4**
investigate	4	L4, U8
invoke	10	L1, U3
involve	**1**	**L2, U3**
isolate	7	L3, U4
issue	1	L4, U2; L0, U8
item	2	L3, U10; L0, U7
job	4	L1, U1
journal	**2**	**L2, U6**
justify	3	L2, U3
label	**4**	**L2, U2**
labor	1	L1, U2
layer	3	L3, U4
lecture	6	L4, U2
legal	**1**	**L2, U3**
legislate	1	L3, U3
levy	**10**	**L2, U9**
liberal	**5**	**L2, U1**
license	5	L3, U9
likewise	10	L4, U5
link	3	L1, U8; L0, U1
locate	**3**	**L2, U1; L0, U1**
logic	5	L1, U6
maintain	2	L4, U1; L0, U9

Word	Sublist	Location
major	1	L3, U2; L0, U5
manipulate	8	L4, U4
manual	9	L3, U10
margin	5	L4, U3
mature	9	L1, U8
maximize	**3**	**L2, U8**
mechanism	4	L3, U9
media	7	L1, U5
mediate	9	L4, U2
medical	5	L1, U2
medium	**9**	**L2, U2**
mental	**5**	**L2, U6**
method	1	L4, U9
migrate	6	L3, U2
military	9	L1, U4
minimal	**9**	**L2, U10**
minimize	8	L1, U1
minimum	6	L4, U5
ministry	6	L1, U2
minor	3	L3, U7
mode	7	L4, U7
modify	**5**	**L2, U3**
monitor	**5**	**L2, U3**
motive	6	L1, U6
mutual	9	L3, U3
negate	3	L4, U2
network	5	L3, U2
neutral	**6**	**L2, U10**
nevertheless	6	L4, U10
nonetheless	10	L4, U7
norm	9	L4, U6
normal	2	L3, U8; L4, U2
notion	5	L4, U9
notwithstanding	**10**	**L2, U1**
nuclear	**8**	**L2, U7**
objective	5	L1, U10
obtain	2	L3, U6; L0, U10
obvious	4	L3, U7
occupy	4	L1, U9
occur	1	L1, U2
odd	10	L1, U8
offset	8	L4, U8
ongoing	10	L3, U3
option	4	L4, U7
orient	**5**	**L2, U5**
outcome	3	L3, U4
output	4	L1, U7
overall	**4**	**L2, U6**
overlap	9	L1, U7

Word	Sublist	Location
overseas	6	L1, U1
panel	10	L1, U6
paradigm	**7**	**L2, U6**
paragraph	8	L3, U6
parallel	4	L3, U9
parameter	4	L4, U5
participate	2	L1, U8
partner	3	L3, U1
passive	**9**	**L2, U8**
perceive	**2**	**L2, U9**
percent	**1**	**L2, U10**
period	**1**	**L2, U6**
persist	**10**	**L2, U4**
perspective	5	L3, U2
phase	4	L1, U8
phenomenon	**7**	**L2, U5**
philosophy	3	L4, U5
physical	3	L4, U4; L0, U4
plus	8	L4, U5
policy	1	L3, U3
portion	9	L3, U9
pose	10	L3, U1
positive	2	L1, U5
potential	2	L4, U8; L0, U10
practitioner	8	L1, U2
precede	**6**	**L2, U4**
precise	5	L3, U10
predict	**4**	**L2, U1**
predominant	8	L1, U8
preliminary	9	L4, U1
presume	**6**	**L2, U2**
previous	**2**	**L2, U5; L0, U5**
primary	2	L1, U1
prime	5	L4, U4
principal	4	L4, U5
principle	1	L3, U9; L0, U9
prior	4	L3, U6
priority	7	L1, U2
proceed	1	L4, U9; L0, U3
process	1	L1, U9
professional	4	L1, U5
prohibit	7	L3, U10
project	4	L4, U4, U9
promote	**4**	**L2, U6**
proportion	3	L1, U10
prospect	**8**	**L2, U6**
protocol	**9**	**L2, U4**
psychology	5	L4, U2
publication	7	L3, U1
publish	3	L1, U3

Oxford 3000™ words

Word	Sublist	Location
🔑 purchase	2	**L2, U9; L0, U7**
🔑 pursue	5	L3, U8
qualitative	9	L3, U9
🔑 quote	7	L4, U10
radical	8	L3, U4
random	8	**L2, U7**
🔑 range	2	L3, U1
🔑 ratio	5	L1, U8
rational	6	L3, U3
🔑 **react**	3	**L2, U6; L0, U3**
🔑 recover	6	L3, U4
refine	9	L4, U4
regime	4	**L2, U10**
🔑 region	2	L3, U1
🔑 **register**	3	**L2, U2**
regulate	2	L3, U6; L0, U9
reinforce	8	**L2, U5**
🔑 reject	5	L1, U7
🔑 relax	9	L1, U8
🔑 release	7	L4, U1
🔑 relevant	2	L4, U8
reluctance	10	**L2, U4**
🔑 rely	3	L3, U2; L0, U6
🔑 remove	3	L3, U2; L0, U8
🔑 require	1	L4, U2; L0, U9
🔑 research	1	L4, U2
reside	2	L1, U2
🔑 resolve	4	L3, U4
🔑 resource	2	L3, U8
🔑 respond	1	L4, U7
🔑 restore	8	L3, U5
restrain	9	**L2, U7**
🔑 **restrict**	2	**L2, U9; L0, U6**
🔑 retain	4	L4, U3
🔑 reveal	6	L3, U8
revenue	5	**L2, U2**
🔑 **reverse**	7	**L2, U7**
🔑 revise	8	L3, U6
🔑 revolution	9	L1, U1
rigid	9	**L2, U7**
🔑 role	1	L1, U5
🔑 **route**	9	**L2, U5**
scenario	9	L3, U7
🔑 schedule	8	L4, U9
scheme	3	L4, U3
scope	6	L4, U8
🔑 **section**	1	**L2, U5**
🔑 sector	1	L1, U3
🔑 secure	2	L4, U6; L0, U8

Word	Sublist	Location
🔑 seek	2	L4, U3; L0, U4
🔑 select	2	L3, U1
sequence	3	L3, U5
🔑 series	4	L3, U5
🔑 sex	3	L1, U3
🔑 shift	3	L4, U9; L0, U2
🔑 significant	1	L3, U10; L0, U6
🔑 **similar**	1	**L2, U1; L0, U2**
simulate	7	L3, U1
🔑 site	2	L1, U6
so-called	10	**L2, U8**
sole	7	L4, U1
🔑 somewhat	7	L1, U4
🔑 source	1	L3, U2; L0, U10
🔑 specific	1	L1, U6
specify	3	L4, U6
sphere	9	L3, U7
🔑 stable	5	L4, U5
statistic	4	L4, U7
🔑 status	4	L3, U2
straightforward	10	L3, U4
🔑 **strategy**	2	**L2, U5; L0, U9**
🔑 stress	4	L4, U4
🔑 **structure**	1	**L2, U1; L0, U5**
🔑 style	5	L1, U4
submit	7	**L2, U9**
subordinate	9	L4, U3
subsequent	4	L1, U1
subsidy	6	**L2, U2**
🔑 substitute	5	L1, U1
successor	7	**L2, U9**
🔑 **sufficient**	3	**L2, U10; L0, U4**
🔑 sum	4	L1, U10
🔑 **summary**	4	**L2, U10**
supplement	9	L4, U10
🔑 survey	2	L1, U3
🔑 survive	7	L3, U2
suspend	9	L1, U10
sustain	5	**L2, U4**
🔑 **symbol**	5	**L2, U2**
🔑 tape	6	L1, U6
🔑 target	5	L3, U10
🔑 task	3	L1, U8
🔑 **team**	9	**L2, U6**
🔑 technical	3	L1, U6
🔑 **technique**	3	**L2, U1; L0, U6**
🔑 technology	3	L3, U8; L0, U7
🔑 temporary	9	L1, U9
tense	8	L1, U10
terminate	8	L1, U9

Word	Sublist	Location
🔑 **text**	2	**L2, U4**
🔑 **theme**	8	**L2, U2**
🔑 theory	1	L4, U4; L0, U9
thereby	8	L4, U3
thesis	7	L4, U7
🔑 topic	7	L3, U3
🔑 trace	6	L1, U9
🔑 tradition	2	L3, U6; L0, U4
🔑 transfer	2	L4, U1; L0, U3
🔑 **transform**	6	**L2, U7**
transit	5	L3, U5
transmit	7	L4, U4
🔑 transport	6	L4, U10; L0, U9
🔑 trend	5	L4, U6
trigger	9	L3, U7
🔑 ultimate	7	L1, U9
undergo	10	L4, U1
underlie	6	L4, U6
undertake	4	**L2, U3**
🔑 uniform	8	L3, U1
unify	9	L4, U5
🔑 **unique**	7	**L2, U1; L0, U7**
utilize	6	L3, U8
🔑 valid	3	L4, U10
🔑 vary	1	L3, U10; L0, U2
🔑 vehicle	8	L4, U3
🔑 version	5	L3, U5
🔑 via	8	L1, U4
violate	9	L3, U6
virtual	8	**L2, U10**
🔑 visible	7	L3, U5
🔑 vision	9	L4, U3
visual	8	L3, U7
🔑 **volume**	3	**L2, U4**
voluntary	7	L1, U10
welfare	5	L4, U1
🔑 whereas	5	L4, U2
whereby	10	L1, U4
widespread	8	L4, U10

🔑 Oxford 3000™ words